Squares, Stripes, and Lice

Squares, Stripes, and Lice

By Ann Kristin Ramstrøm, editor,

Hanne Dale and Siri Angela Gamborg

TRAFALGAR SQUARE
North Pomfret, Vermont

First published in the United States of America
in 2020 by
Trafalgar Square Books
North Pomfret, Vermont 05053

Originally published in Norwegian as *Ruter og lus: Retrostrikk frå Salhus Tricotage fabrik.*

This book project received support from the municipality of Belgium, Norway.

ISBN: 978-1-64601-020-2
Library of Congress Control Number: 2020940129

Interior Graphic Design Type-it AS
Cover Photo Tove Lise Mossestad
Norwegian Publisher's Editor Laila.andreassen@museumsforlaget.no
Translation into English Carol Huebscher Rhoades

Printed in China
10 9 8 7 6 5 4 3 2 1

Table of Contents

Museums are filled with all kinds of treasures: beautiful artifacts, exciting stories, and intriguing facts about our ancestors and how they lived their lives. These things give us a glimpse into the past, and those of us who work in museums love to share those objects and their history.

A little outside Bergen, Norway, you'll find a former textile mill, Salhus Tricotagefabrik (Salhus Knitting Factory), which began producing everyday garments in 1859. All the way until 1989, the knitting machines produced yard after yard of fabric, to be sewn into everyday garments for adults and children. These everyday clothes also had to look nice, and even the simplest knitting machines were able to produce attractive geometric patterns to embellish clothing that was then constructed by seamstresses at the factory.

The copious pattern archive of knitted samples saved from the Salhus factory contains some irreplaceable textile work, and that's what we want to showcase in this book. Although clothing is no longer produced there, luckily it didn't take long before the site was included on the Norwegian Directoate for Culturla Heritage (Riksantikvaren) list of selected industrial heritage sites. Today, the factory is a national reminder of the history of the Norwegian textile industry, and is home to the Norwegian Knitting Industry Museum (Norsk Trikotasjemuseum); we take care of the buildings, machines, archives, and objects from the Salhus factory.

In museums, we often bring out our finest artifacts for an exhibit; this time, you can take them home, in a book with newly designed clothing inspired by vintage knitted patterns we hope you'll like. Some of the foremost Norwegian knitwear designers have contributed to this book. They took on the challenge with open arms, and, based on machine-worked designs from Salhus, they've created patterns for new cardigans and pullovers, dresses, and interior furnishings.

Remembering factory workers who, many decades ago, ran what were then cutting-edge knitting machines and brought forth these simple but attractive patterns, we are proud to have adapted their work into striking modern knitwear that primarily uses Norwegian-produced yarn. The garments are named for company trademarks and brands, and for some of the women and men who worked in production at the Salhus factory. This is how we honor our factory workers!

Without my good colleagues Hanne Dale and Siri Angela Gamborg, I doubt that this book would have been published. Thankfully, they saw how important it was to show the knitting motifs that inspired us to develop this concept for producing a knitting book. Thank you to those who knitted test swatches and, not least, to Hanne Dale again, for wielding your pen through the book and untangling on all the threads of instructions, stitch counts, and conversations with designers—everything that must take place before a book can go to press.

We also wish to thank Hillesvåg Ullvarefabrikk, Rauma Garn, and Sandnes Garn for their wonderful Norwegian-produced yarns, most of them spun with Norwegian wool, provided to us for these patterns. Thank you to all the test knitters who were up early and late to knit the finished garments for this book. A big thank you to the lovely models who went out in their free time and made the garments look as fine as they do! Thanks also to photographer Tove Lise Mossestad, make-up artist Seline Rasmussen Bjørseth, and editor Laila Andreassen.

We hope you enjoy these brand-new handknit garments filled with history!

Ann Kristin Ramstrøm
Director, Norwegian Knitting Industry Museum

The Beginnings of a Knitting Adventure: Salhus Tricotagefabrik (1859-1989)

A new time was imminent, a new time of both good and evil, like other ages which had come before. It was a time of singing wheels and smoking factory chimneys, a time of both condemnation and praise for industrialization. [...] The new rhythm came from England, where the smoke from the factory chimneys had long stoked the green meadows [...] The new time arrived in Salhus in 1859, with the building of the knitting factory and the man who took the initiative to do it, Phillip Christian Clausen from Broager in Schleswig.[1]

Welcome to Salhus: a small company town just north of Bergen. For a long time, there were three textile factories active here, with around 700 employees. But back when Phillip Christian Clausen and dye master Johan Ernst Christian Ramm laid the foundation for the first textile factory, there was scarcely a house to see. The lease was signed in August 1859 and the factory building for the firm of J. Ramm & Clausen was ready before the year's end. The town began to grow up around it, bit by bit.

Founders from Schleswig

Production began at a measured pace, with two knitting machines, one sewing machine, and one machine for winding and plying yarn.[2] The two founders had gone to study at Arne Fabrikker in Ytre Arna, where Peter Jensen had already founded Norway's first mechanical cotton weaving factory in 1846. Ramm was the dye master in Arna before he went into partnership with Clausen. Clausen himself had a basic education in textile production under Jebsen when he came to Bergen in 1853, when he was 16 years old. Later, he received further training in England.[3]

The textile industry was among the first modern industries to be established in Norway. Hordaland became a core region in the business, with heavyweights of the day such as the Arne, Janus, and Dale factories. Many of these factories produced knitted clothing, or "tricotage." Salhus Tricotagefabrik and O. A. Devold (1853-1988) in Møre og Romsdal became the country's first fully mechanized knitting factories, and were part of the first wave of industrialization. Many of the textile factories around Bergen sprung from business ventures of Peter Jebsen's family and acquaintances from Schleswig, on the border between Germany and Denmark.

In the beginning, the new knitting factory in Salhus bought finished yarn for their knitwear, but in 1863, they invested in their own steam engine and machines for carding and spinning. Many of the earlier textile factories were situated by rivers, from Aker River (Akerselva) in Oslo to Blindheim River in Ytre Arna, and used water power to run their machines. In Salhus, there was no river large enough for that—but the area was otherwise suitable, and there was good access to cheap labor. During the first decade the factory was in operation, production was simple and partly driven by

North Salhus with the factory in about 1900. The factory was built up in many stages over the years. The original factory building from 1859 was replaced by a new wooden building in 1910, but the workers' residences from around 1860 remain.

Workers at Salhus Tricotagefabrik in 1890, with director Philip Christian Clausen and his son Emil Clausen at the center of the photo.

hand, but after a while, the factory obtained a stronger steam engine and built up its belt operations for the machines in several stages. There were between 50 and 60 workers in the factory in the second half of the nineteenth century. Most of the workers were women, but many men worked in the early stages of the production process, i.e., carding and spinning yarn, which was heavy, dirty labor. There were also men who tended knitting machines, while women wound yarn, sewed, and folded and assessed the finished garments.

Krone Wool Keeps You Warm

Ramm and Clausen also ran a flour and grain business, but after a failed investment, J. Ramm & Clausen went into bankruptcy in 1888. This, in turn, affected the knitting factory, which also failed. Machines, facilities, and houses were put up for sale—and then, that same year, the business was re-organized as the corporation Salhus Tricotagefabrik under Philip Christian Clausen. He moved to Salhus with his family and devoted himself fully to the factory business. During the next decade, the factory and machinery were modernized. By about 1920, most of the machines were driven by electric motors.[4] Business was good and, in the 1930s, the number of employees increased to over 200.

Salhus Tricotagefabrik became recognized all around Norway for its durable everyday clothing: wool sweaters, wool socks, underwear, and sports clothes. Cotton undergarments under the brand name Krone Maco eventually became classics, and the factory continued to produce clothing for 130 years.[5]

From Wool to Undergarments

Production began with intake of wool, sorting, and washing. Later, the wool was blended with other fibers, and spinning oil and water were added before it was ready for carding. The factory used both Norwegian and imported wool, and up until the 1950s, farmers in the district sold wool directly to the factory. The imported wool came, in large part, from Australia and New Zealand. Waste wool and yarn from production was shredded and re-used,

but the factory also bought large amounts of waste fibers (rags, filler, and shoddy [6]) to process. In 1930, they processed 7,500 kilos of Norwegian wool, 18,200 kilos of imported wool, 37,000 kilos of cotton and a total of 77,000 kilos of waste fiber. They also bought cellulose-based synthetics (viscose). Up until 1947, the factory spun its own wool and cotton yarn; after that, only wool yarn was spun at Salhus.[7]

The next steps in the yarn production process are carding, spinning, and winding onto bobbins. Carding machines have large drums with metal needles that blend and comb fibers so they all lie in the same direction. At the end of the carding process, wool is drawn out into pencil roving, which is then transferred to spinning machines. Roving is then stretched into yarn, plied, and wound onto bobbins. Spooled yarn is rewound onto waxed paper cones, which can hold more yarn than the original bobbins. This happens on a winding machine. Finished yarn was used to knit fabric, either in a single color or patterned. Various parts of garments were cut out using paper templates (*skantar*) in different sizes. These cut-out fabric pieces were then passed on to the seamstresses, who sewed the garments together before they were labeled, checked, and packed. Dyeing could occur at differing stages of the process. The wool fiber could be dyed after washing, or as finished yarn, or as finished knitted fabric, if it was to be a single color.

A Tight-Knit Industrial Society

The factory was situated by the coast just north of central Bergen, with good harbor access for transportation by sea. A road was not built until 1928, but a coastal steamer route was already in place by 1864. Salhus is well-located, and the first stop for boats on the way from Bergen. On the hill behind the factory, a tight-knit community grew with houses both for workers and managers, a schoolhouse, and an old-age home.

From 1850 until today, Salhus experienced the same big cultural and economic changes as in Norway in general: the shift from a farming community to modern industrialization. The textile industry in Hordaland

The Norwegian word *trikotasje* comes from the French *tricoter*, which means "to knit." The word is used in reference to machine-knitted fabrics and garments, and the industry that produced them, as equivalent to *trikot*.

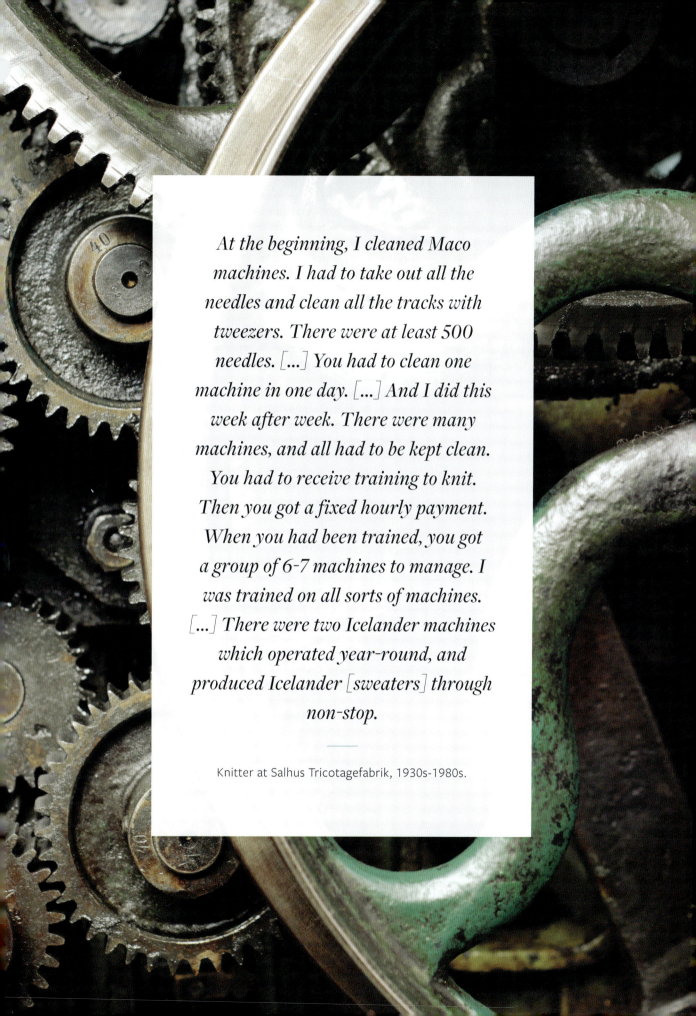

At the beginning, I cleaned Maco machines. I had to take out all the needles and clean all the tracks with tweezers. There were at least 500 needles. [...] You had to clean one machine in one day. [...] And I did this week after week. There were many machines, and all had to be kept clean. You had to receive training to knit. Then you got a fixed hourly payment. When you had been trained, you got a group of 6-7 machines to manage. I was trained on all sorts of machines. [...] There were two Icelander machines which operated year-round, and produced Icelander [sweaters] through non-stop.

Knitter at Salhus Tricotagefabrik, 1930s-1980s.

Well, we mainly talked about sewing: [...] "You know what? Today, it's gone totally haywire because there were so many things went wrong." So then you ruin the piecework rate you've built up and that one day can bring you right down. [...] But as a rule, we maintained a good rate of work. You worked hard, you felt good about it, and we managed.
Seamstress at Salhus Tricotagefabrik, in the 1960s.

became important for developing business life in the region and for several neighboring towns, and Salhus is an example. It's easy to draw lines to other nearby towns outside the biggest cities which were built up around a central core business. The textile industry included the Dale factory in Vaksdal, the Berger factory in Vestfold, and Solberg Spinneri by Solbergelva at Drammen.

Salhus grew from being a small tourist town on the way out of Bergen to a busy industrial town with two knitwear factories: Salhus Tricotagefabrik and Birkelund Trikotasjefabrikk (1920-1959) and a weavin mill, Salhaus Vœverier (1894-1997).

It was a compact community; the town and the factory were two sides of the same coin. The industry provided the basis for a rich variety of social activities, especially in sports and music. The city was later known for its reviews and popular music from the 1950s onwards, played by local bands such as Salhuskvintetten. Salhus also saw good times in the 1960s, but then the town suffered in a general downturn of the Norwegian textile industry, due to increased globalization and imports from low-wage countries. In 1989, Salhus Tricotagefabrik closed down—13 years after a neighboring business, Salhus Vœverier, had done the same.

Just before, the smoke from the factory chimneys stopped, the plant was assessed for conservation as an example of the textile industry in western Norway. The factory became part of the Directorate for Cultural Heritage conservation program for technical industries of cultural heritage in 1997, and today it is the only national industry heritage site in Bergen. Now, the Norwegian Knitting Industrial Museum resides within the factory buildings, and showcases the history of the Norwegian textile industry based on these industrial buildings. In 2020, the factory site will be entirely protected.

Paper templates, or *skantar*, were used to cut out garment pieces; these are for sleeveless undershirts (1975).

I started out working in the sewing department. We stood, cutting out neckbands for the undershirts. You were assigned light work before you began to sew. Then you got a percentage; you didn't get much but it stimulated you to work so that you could earn a little extra. Once they saw how you performed, you might be moved around from one job to another. There were seasons for different types of clothing. I was often moved from one department to another.

Seamstress at Salhus Tricotagefabrik, 1950s-80s.

Above: Seamstresses in one of the factory sewing rooms in 1976.
Below: Winding the yarn onto paper cones, in about the 1950s.

Top: Salhus with the Norwegian Knitting Industry Museum in the center of the photo, and the former weaving mill Salhus Vœverier in the background.

Below: Salhus Tricotagefabrik as seen from the seaside.

18

I am neither a baron nor a count but underclothes with a Crown (Krone), I require. (Slogan for Krone Tricotage, 1935)

Sketch for the Krone logo in the factory archives.

"Place a crown on the work!
Krone (Crown)
Registered trademark
Ask for
The Krone brand"

To "put a crown on" is a Norwegian idiom, meaning to
add a finishing touch, to complete to a hish standear

The Crown of the Works: Production at Salhus Tricotagefabrik

The Krone pattern, you choose with ease;

the shape and color make it a breeze

for every woman our advertising might please.

The light and airy summer clothes

are fine as silk but strong as ropes.

We have the strength and Krone brand for our clothes.

For first prize we will always compete;

our Krone brand offers the rest defeat.

So, if you're listening, and think of purchasing,

remember us.

— Radio advertisement for Salhus, Tricotagefabrik, read by poet Herman Wildenwey, 1935.

Over its lifetime, Salhus Tricotagefabrik produced everything from long underwear to men's briefs, "Icelander" sweaters[8], and sports clothes. Wool and cotton men's underwear, wool socks, and sweaters were the core products for a long time. In 1925, the factory registered what would become its most recognized trademark: Krone Tricotage.[9] In the 1930s, undergarments branded as Krone Opal, Lino, Sefyr (Zephyr), Sakel, Asjur, and Olympic came onto the market, as well as brands named for gemstones: Rubin (Ruby), Safir (Sapphire), Agat (Agate), and Topas (Topaz).

Work Clothing and Undergarments

More than anything else, the factory produced undergarments: tops and bottoms, long and short, in wool and cotton. In the 1890s, the most important products were men's shirts, work sweaters, and trousers. Little had changed 30 years later. In 1921, men's sweaters, men's trousers, and stockings were the most-produced items. The factory also made smaller amounts of garments such as women's garments, gymnastics clothing, swimsuits, football outfits, and abdominal belts. October to January were the busiest months, while it was calmest in July. Overall, cotton garments sold in the largest quatities.[9]

They did still produce large quantities of wool socks, and by 1896, Salhus Tricotagefabrik had already purchased Norway's first automatic circular sock knitting machine. Sixty years later, in 1959, the factory acquired Birkelund Trikotasjefabrikk in Salhus and transferred its sock production there.

Maco-mania

All-cotton undergarments made with Egyptian Maco cotton became a popular product, as well as "winter-Maco" lined with terrycloth. The factory tried to register "Winter Maco" and "Summer Maco" as brand names in 1913, but met resistance from their competitor Pedersen and Dekke, who contended that they could not trademark a type of cotton. After a while, Maco became such a common word that it could no longer be considered as a brand name. In 1919, the director, Emil Clausen, traveled to the United States to study and he bought American Cooper knitting machines, which were used to knit what became the most recognized brand: Krone ("Crown") Maco.

The factory's first big advertising campaign kicked off in 1935, aiming to establish Krone Maco as a brand name in Norway. Before then, Salhus Tricotagefabrik had done very little advertising of its products. The company had participated in several industry and merchandise exhibitions and received honorable mentions in Stockholm, Drammen, and Paris by the 1860s and 70s, bronze in Stockholm in 1897, and silver in Bergen in 1898. But by 1935, their competitors had begun to put money into marketing and in Salhus one would be foolish not to advertise. The campaign for Krone-Maco included short radio ads with the poet Herman Wildenwey, placards and ads in newspapers, and at movie theaters. The ads portrayed Krone garments as durable—and therefore economical—well-fitting underclothes that were popular in all social classes. They sponsored a competition for a brand motto and first prize went to the motto: "Put a crown on the work—ask for the Krone trademark."

Airy Solutions

Theories about a possible connection between good underclothing and physical wellbeing led to the production of "health clothing," with the idea that an insulating airiness near the skin helped to hold in warmth. Dovre was the first to release "health vests"—arriving on the market late in the 1930s, hand-knitted by these were women who had this as their home industry work. In

Opplagt hele året i **KRONE OLYMPIC** *Helseundertøy*

Ad for Krone Olympic "health vests," with matching underpants.

1960 came the first machine-knitted "health clothing" from Dovre. The company Brynje and EKT (Edvin K. Thorson) began production of "health" underclothing soon after the Second World War.[11]

We aren't certain exactly when they began producing health clothing in Salhus, but such garments were a popular product by 1950. In the years following, other products were developed with the same fabric, such as Maco undershirts with health gussets under the arms, and similarly styled underpants. The products were playfully compared with Viking chainmail in the ads. And who wouldn't want to wear one, after that?

Fine-spun golden coats of mail had those Nordic gods
in Valhalla, the home of the gods.
Nowadays, daughters and sons,

Ad from the 1980s.

*Every man feels in Olympic form with Krone-Maco.
Because good underclothing gives a feeling of well-being,
and is a primary condition for robust health. Therefore, it
is safe to say that Krone Maco and good health go hand-
in-hand.*
(Radio ad for Salhus Tricotagefabrik in 1935)

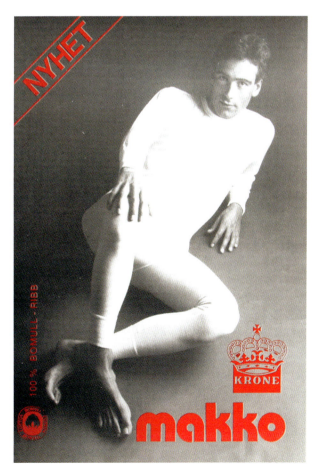

in modern as well as ordinary homes,
city people as well as farmers,
will find their chainmail at Salhus.
It's lighter, but with as much staying power
as the chainmail of yesterday's berserker.
With the crown on it, it's all-powerful,
and the price is quite affordable.

*(Radio advertisement for Salhaus Tricotagefabrik,
read by Herman Wildenwey in 1935.)*

Underclothing Ready for the Light of Day

After the 1950s, Maco material was gradually replaced by interlock, a thick fabric with two layers of thread, so both the front and back of the fabric were alike. In the decades following, several new products appeared in synthetic fibers.

In line with the times, in 1968, Salhus Tricotagefabrik launched cotton undergarments with printed patterns for the first time, printed by Martens Fabrikker in Denmark. The colors were an intense orange, turquoise, and red; and in the 1970s, they also produced brown, purple, and pink undergarments. These were a huge success, but also to a large degree a fashion item. The factory worked three shifts making undergarments but that wasn't enough to meet demand.

Protection Against the Elements

"Icelander" sweaters, fishermen's sweaters, or work sweaters (different terms for the handweaving in Salhus) had a classic, straight silhouette and wide or slightly flared sleeves. The oldest styles didn't have ribbing, but rather a section in a lighter color at the lower part of the sweater, and a boat neck or tie closure at the neckline. Later, they changed to sewn-on, doubled ribbed bands at the neck, sleeve cuffs, and bottom edge of the sweaters. Most of these garments had patterns in two or three colors, many of which were common hand-knitting motifs and from other producers such as Devold, Petersen and Dekke, and Janus.

Wool sweaters in red and black, or natural white and brown or gray, were the most common at Salhus Tricotagefabrik. Repeats were generally small, and the motifs simple and geometric, usually repeated over a large surface. These small, multi-color motifs made a better fabric—warmer and more durable. The fabric for the "Icelander" sweaters was knitted on large circular knitting machines, and then cut out to form sleeves and body by following paper templates. Ribbing was knitted on separate machines and then sewn on.

Early in the 1950s, production went well and "Icelander" sweaters were a popular item. The factory sought patent protection for several trademarks with Icelandic references: Geysir ("geyser"), Snorre, and Hekla. Later in the 1960s, demand lessened and stripes were added to the ribbing to modernize the garment. In the 1970s, "Icelanders" were once again in style and became an export product. By 1973, the demand was so great that spinning and knitting had to be outsourced to other manufacturers in order to satisfy the market. Salhus saw the opportunity to take over Kvinge Wool Spinnery in Masfjorden to increase capacity, but decided to invest on their own spinnery instead.

Sports Clothing and Hard Times

Salhus produced more and more sports clothing in the post-war period: jackets, pullovers, training suits, sports socks, and swimsuits. The factory provided training outfits for the Norwegian Olympic teams, and in 1982, Cobra was launched as a new trademark for sports clothes. The factory also produced profile garments such as college sweaters and graduation clothes. The archives show that around this time, the company had employees responsible for sales and for the compilation of a coherent collection, who traveled to fashion exhibits, and made an effort to follow the fashions—but this may have been too little, too late.

At the same time, it was becoming increasingly hard to make a profit, and around 1980 the factory had to bring in consultants to analyze the situation. As the '80s continued, the number of employees was gradually reduced, and efforts were made to cut costs

Gode råd mot dårlig kondis.

Først anskaffer du en skikkelig treningsdrakt. Salhus har en utmerket sådan. Krone i 100 % crepenylon. Holder fasongen, selv etter gjentatte turer i vaskemaskinen. Overdelen er rød, buksen blå.

Så begynner du å spise litt mindre. Og deretter legger du opp et treningsprogram som du tror du blir passe sliten av. Legg inn noen øvelser som du synes er morsomme å gjøre. Begynn forsiktig, øk etterhvert som formen kommer seg. Og husk, noen minutter hver dag er bedre enn skippertak, en gang i mellom.

Hvorfor ikke gi dine kunder de samme tipsene? I alle fall kan du trygt anbefale Krone treningsdrakt. Og ta godt i når du bestiller. Folk har begynt å skjønne at det er lurt å holde seg i form.

KRONE *treningsdrakt*

Det er godt det finnes undertøy som tåler dagens lys

Undertøyet er en privatsak som man vanligvis ikke løper rundt i. Men i Krones kulørte undertøy føler man seg litt friere, fordi man faktisk ser mer påkledd ut. Det er ikke så farlig om noen skulle se hva man har på seg innerst inne. Krones kulørte undertøy tåler dagens lys. Både truse og T-shirt leveres i alle størrelser og i tre farger: blått, rødt og orange. Plaggene er laget av 100 % bomull, og de er farge-ekte slik at de kan kokes. Strikken i trusen er utskiftbar. Til Krones kulørte undertøy hører også lange og knekorte underbenklær. Bestill i dag. Og kalkuler med at de fleste vil ha undertøy som tåler dagens lys. Krone.

Underclothes were no longer "unmentionables" that had to be hidden. This ad from 1972 suggests that the new underwear, in color prints, looks so good it could be worn on its own.

The knitting department at Salhus Tricotagefabrik around the 1930s. Factory director Emil Clausen, inspired by a 1919 study tour in the United States, invested in the American Cooper knitting machines shown here to produce the factory's signature Krone Maco underclothing. The machines were driven by belts from the ceiling and knitted "upwards" so the finished fabric rolled up at the top. It was heavy work to lift down the finished rolls; this was regarded as men's labor.

and increase efficiency, but it wasn't enough. As the remnants of the textile industry began to disappear from Salhus, the factory building gained new life as "Norsk Trikotasjemuseum og Tekstilsenter" (Norwegian Knitting Industry Museum and Textile Center). The museum was founded in 1992, and officially opened in 2001, replacing the industry that had once sprung from nothing and transitioning once more to a new era.

for home use produced knitted goods for sale and provided a good source of extra income for many women in the second half of the nineteenth century and into the twentieth century.[12] "Icelander" motifs from hand-knitting tradition were adapted by factories and mass-produced in the latter half of the nineteenth century—and now we're taking them back into our own hands, needles, and yarn.

Squares and Lice: Pattern Motifs at the Factory

The first knitting machines at the factory were manual circular knitting machines with hand-driven cranks; later came belt- and steam-driven machines, and finally those with electric motors. It's a little ironic that we're now adapting patterns from machine-knitted meterage to hand knitting. But machine- and hand-knitting have existed side by side since the first knitting factories were established in the middle of the nineteenth century. Simple flatbed and circular knitting machines

Red, White, and Blue—and Gray

Fabric samples and archive materials give us an insight into how motifs and colors have changed over the years. We know little about the patterns in use in the nineteenth century, but they were probably similar to those in production later: white cotton and wool undergarments, stockings, and heavy wool work sweaters. Production shifted gradually to finer-quality fabric, as the machinery was modernized. Around the turn of the century, we find many stripe patterns and two-color wool sweaters with lice and simple geometric motifs.

Hjemmeindustri A/S (Home Industry Company) sold knitting machines in the 1920s-40s and promised good supplementary incomes because they also bought the finished knitted goods. The head office was on Jernbanetorget (Railway Square) in Oslo but the company also had divisions in Bergen, Stavanger, Trondheim, Narvik, and Harstad.

The knitting samples from around 1900 in bright pink and purple are perhaps a little more surprising, while patterns in red, white, and blue are a constant.

In the 1920s and 30s, gray and beige heather samples dominate, usually with pattern colors of brown, blue, and yellow. At that time, burgundy, blue, gray, and soft greens slipped into the color palette. The heathers could have been spun from natural variations in sheep's wool, several combined strands, or perhaps recycled textile fibers, or shoddy—wool fabric that was shredded and re-spun. There are some relief-stitch patterns in the archives, mostly in finer fabrics that might have been used for stockings. These were normally single-color, while heavier wool garments were knitted in in several colors.

Gradual Development

Many of the patterns would have been used for several years in a row and appear to have been developed over time through that use. It's only in later decades that evidence surfaces of a design department, and actual drawings of garments are found in the archives. Before that, there had long been a tailor or designer at the factory who had responsibility for shaping new garments and perhaps also the patterning on the fabric.

New patterns could have been developed by making small changes in the programming of the knitting machine. Simply changing a couple of stitches of a row in a pattern or choosing new colors could result in a totally different look. Icelanders and heavy work sweaters often had patterns with variations of simple lice, diagonal and horizontal stripes, and squares. The same fabric could be used for simple V-neck knitted sweater-jackets.

The fabric patterns were not created in a vacuum—the factory used common motifs and was also influenced by fashion, other factories, and hand-knitting. There were many variations of the diamond-shaped "Argyle" pattern, for example, starting in the mid-1930s. The pattern, which originated in Scottish woven textiles, was popular in England after the first World War and was later adapted for knitted garments, such as vests, sweaters, and socks. The eight-petaled rose,

Heathered fabrics and "Argyle" diamond patterns on knitted samples from 1932-35.

common in Norwegian hand knitting, pops up in several places, and we can see inspiration from Faroese fishermen's sweaters and small-motif knitted garments in many "Icelander" fabrics.

There are many simple stripe patterns in the knitted samples from early in the twentieth century, several of which call to mind the Norwegian flag.

I knew and liked the "Icelander" machines best, I was most in sync with them. It was more calming somehow: how many machines you had and how you cared for them and made sure they worked. It was an art. Oiling them, and every day we had to blow and brush them clean before we started. On the newest machines, I could knit three 13-kilo lengths on a shift.

Knitter at Salhus Tricotagefabrik, 1930s-80s.

From Samples to Garments

Salhus Tricotagefabrik had a rich history of clothing production, and we have many examples of patterns that were used for knitted sweaters in the museum's storage sections and archives. Our work on this book began with a desire to show off the factory's work and these patterns in a new way and to reach a new audience.

The patterns contained here are based on whole garments, knitted samples, ads, and other materials from Salhus. Among other items in the archives from the Salhus Tricotagefabrik, we found dated knitted samples from the early twentieth century all the way up to the 1980s. With the help of a group of good designers, these small samples were turned into patterns for new sweaters, cardigans, and dresses which we believe you'll love. You'll find both classic "Icelanders" and interior decoration pieces, skirts, and dresses: garments with small motifs and a simple geometric look.

We've chosen patterns from various time periods in the factory's history that we hope will appeal to today's knitters. There are few sources, from the first forty years of the factory's operation, so we've focused on the period after 1900. We decided not to use some of the most common "Icelander" motifs, as these are used in many other knitting patterns. Other "Icelander" sweaters from after the second World War up to the 1980s are shown in the book, together with other patterns from the early twentieth century. Even though most of the designs feature stranded color-work patterning, they are relatively easy to knit, with small pattern repeats and never more than two colors per round. Many of the pullovers have raglan shaping instead of set-in sleeves, a feature which ensures a good fit and makes finishing easier.

Our starting point was primarily the heavier fabric for wool pullovers, since those were the samples in the archives most suitable for hand-knitting. Many of the knitting machines in the factory had long needles that were smaller in circumference than anything that could be purchased in a knitting shop. Some of the structure in machine-knitted "Icelanders" would be difficult to recreate by hand, because machines knit differently than people. Machine knitting gives a different structure and prominence to certain stitches; stockinette stitch worked in the round by hand is smooth and flat. In some instances, we changed motifs slightly to make them easier to hand-knit.

Our work started with a choice of motifs and sketches of pattern charts. Some of the samples were easy to follow; others were worn and felted with age, and had been mounted on pieces of cardboard with glue. At the beginning, we tried to find yarns and colors similar to those in the originals, but the designers were free to choose new colors. Some motifs are featured on entirely new types of projects; others embellish smart, stylish pullovers and cardigans, one of the most common categories of garments made at the factory.

Designers

Birger Berge is a historian and knitting designer based in Bergen, Norway, with an ever-increasing passion for knitting. He finds inspiration everywhere—in nature, from other knitters, in various techniques, and from vintage garments and patterns, such as those from Salhus Tricotagefabrik. He is the author of *Nordic Knits with Birger Berge*.

Siv Kari Dyvik is an established knitwear designer with 20 years' experience in the Norwegian knitting industry. Since 2015, she has worked as a freelance designer and pattern writer and has worked on several best-selling books. She moved to London in 2016 and now works from there with patterns, yarn, and knitting needles.

Berit Løkken is the in-house designer for Hillesvåg Ullvarefabrikk. She has 20 years' experience as a designer for hand knits. She combines design work and shop management at the mill in Lindås outside Bergen. She likes to work with colors and loves to discover someone wearing one of her designs.

Birte Sandvik is a cultural historian and conservator at the Norwegian Folk Museum. She was the project leader for the permanent exhibition "Knitting in Norway" at the Folk Museum in 2013. In 2015, she and her sister Margareth Sandvik published their knitting book *Rett på tråden* [*Knitting with the Sandvik Sisters*], with their own colorful designs.

Margareth Sandvik is a Professor of Norwegian at the Oslo Met—Oslo Metropolitan University. In 2015, she and her sister, Birte Sandvik, published their knitting book, *Rett på tråden* [*Knitting with the Sandvik Sisters*], with their own colorful designs.

Dianna Walla is a knitting designer living in Trondheim, Norway. After having lived in northern Norway for two years, she developed a great interest in Norwegian wool and the Norwegian cultural landscape.

Kristin Wiola Ødegård has published five books with Gyldendal Press in Norway, and is the author of *Scandinavian Sweaters*. "Wiola," as she's known for her design work, usually features non-traditional colors in her designs, and likes to combine various techniques in a single garment. For her, handwork is absolutely essential for feeling good: it's simultaneously creative and a source of inner peace.

Yarn

In this book, we used wool and alpaca yarns from Hillesvåg Ullvarefabrikk, Rauma Garn, and Sandnes Garn, three spinning mills producing yarn in Norway. We have primarily used Norwegian wool for these designs, from classics such as Sandnes Garn's Peer Gynt to the many color choices of Rauma's Finull, and Ask from Hillesvåg.

Hillesvåg Ullvarefabrikk is a mill on the Oster Fjord outside Bergen, Norway with roots going back to 1898. The mill produces yarn for hand- and machine-knitting, with a focus on Norwegian. Hillesvåg is a wool family-run business with strong handwork traditions and yarn production through four generations. In 2013, the mill was given the status of an Econo-museum, connecting to a network of handcrafters with a focus on quality who foster traditional handcraft techniques. Visitors to the yarn shop can tour the mill and experience the production process close up.

From Hillesvåg, we have used Norwegian wool yarn—including the *pels* (pelt) wool yarns Tinde and Sølje, and the lamb's-wool yarns Sol and Vilje. Norwegian pelt wool comes from a Norwegian sheep breeds with light and dark gray wavy wool fibers. These sheep graze outdoors most of the year, and have a soft, lustrous wool. Pelt sheep have medium gray as their natural color, and are the starting point for 30 heathered colors. The yarn can be combined with lighter colors of lamb's wool: Tinde works well with Sol, and Sølje with Vilje. In the patterns, you'll also find Troll woolen yarn, which is a heavier two-ply yarn, and Ask (Hifa 2), a two-ply woolen yarn which is available in a wide range of colors that offers many possibilities for multi-color designs.

Norwegian wool yarns:
- Ask, 2-ply woolen-spun yarn, 344 yd/315 m / 100 g, needles U. S. 1.5-8 / 2.5-5 mm.
- Embla, 3-ply woolen-spun yarn, 230 yd/ 210 m / 100 g, needles U. S. 4-6 / 3.5-4 mm.
- Norsk Villsaugarn (Norwegian wild sheep yarn), 2-ply woolen yarn, 246 yd/225 m / 100 g, needles U. S. 6 / 4 mm.
- Troll, 2-ply woolen-spun yarn, 125 yd/114 m / 100 g, needles U. S. 9-10 / 5.5-6 mm.
- Bonde, 3-ply sock yarn, 80% Norwegian wool, 20% nylon, 183 yd/167 m / 100 g, needles U. S. 4-6 / 3.5-4 mm.
- Fjell sokkegarn (sock yarn), 3-ply woolen-spun yarn, 80% Norwegian wool, 20% nylon, 183 yd/ 167 m/ 100 g, needles U. S. 4-6 / 3.5-4 mm.
- Fjord sokkegarn (sock yarn), 2-ply woolen-spun yarn, 80% Norwegian wool, 20% nylon, 273 yd/250 m / 100 g, needles U. S. 1.5-2.5 / 2.5-3 mm.
- Sol lamullgarn (lamb's wool yarn), 2-ply woolen-spun yarn, 317 yd/290 m / 100 g, needles U. S. 4-6 / 3.5-4 mm.
- Vilje lamullgarn (lamb's wool yarn), 2-ply woolen-spun yarn, 410 yd/375 m / 100 g, needles U. S. 2.5 / 3 mm.
- Blåne pelsullgarn (pelt sheep's wool yarn), 2-ply woolen-spun yarn, 125 yd/114 m / 100 g, needles U. S. 10 / 6 mm. Combines well with Troll.
- Sølje pelsullgarn (pelt sheep's wool yarn), 2-ply woolen-spun yarn, 383 yd/350 m / 100 g, needles U. S. 2.5 / 3 mm.
- Tinde pelsullgarn (pelt sheep's wool yarn), 2-ply woolen yarn, 284 yd/260 m / 100 g, needles U. S. 4-6 / 3.5-4 mm.

Rauma Garn was established in 1927 along the river Rauma at Veblungsnes in Møre and Romsdal, Norway. In 1968, Rauma acquired Røros Tweed and consolidated all the yarn production at Rauma. Røros Tweed was developed as a modern weaving mill, which today produces Røros blankets and fabric for bunads, traditional folk costumes. In 1998, Rauma also acquired the yarn distributor Per Tryving AS and today sells the yarn under the brand Rauma Yarn as PT yarn.

From Rauma, we have used Finullgarn, a two-ply woolen yarn available in many colors—perfect for making your own mark on a knitting project! The yarn, made with Norwegian wool, is also good for felting, producing light and soft fabrics after washing. We also worked with Tumi, a soft three-ply 50/50 wool/alpaca yarn.

Norwegian wool yarns:
- 3-tråds strikkegarn (knitting yarn), 118 yd/ 108 m / 50 g, needles U. S. 4 / 3.5 mm.
- Finull PT2, 2-ply, 191 yd/175 m / 50 g, needles U. S. 1.5-4 / 2.5-3.5 mm.
- Vamsegarn, 2-ply, 91 yd/83 m / 50 g, needles U. S. 10-10½ / 6-6.5 mm.
- Røros lamullgarn (lamb's-wool yarn), 2-ply woolen-spun yarn, approx. 273 yd/250 m / 50 g, needles U. S. 1.5 / 2.5 mm.
- 2-ply Gammelserie (old series), 175 yd/160 m / 50 g, needles U. S. 1.5 / 2.5 mm.
- 4-ply Spælsaugarn, 164 yd/150 m / 50 g, needles U. S. 6 / 4 mm.

Sandnes Garn originated as Sandnes Uldvarefabrik in the center of Sandnes, Norway in 1888. Peer Gynt and Sandhill Tweed are two well-known brands from the mill, which, at its height, had over 500 employees. The business merged with Sandnes Kamgarn Spinnery in 1975 and continued both brand lines. In 1980, the company moved to Foss-Eikeland outside Sandnes, because the mill in Sandnes burned down in 1978. In 1995, Sandnes was sold to Sagatex, but five years later was bought back by new local owners.

In 2006, the firm changed its name to Sandnes Garn and has since focused on producing hand-knitting yarn. Sandnes Garn is the largest yarn mill in Norway and today exports to Denmark, Sweden, and Iceland. The mill produces both worsted- and woolen-spun wool yarns and sells cotton and alpaca yarns that are wound, skeined, and dyed in the mill.

Among other yarns for this book, we've used Peer Gynt, a classic worsted-spun Norwegian wool yarn that has had its own brand since 1938 and is great for sweaters and large garments. Fritidsgarn, also spun from Norwegian wool, is a heavier yarn that works well for felting, but can also be used for larger garments. Additionally, we've knitted with soft alpaca yarns: Alpakka and the thinner Mini Alpakka. Mini Alpakka can also be substituted with Sisu (80% wool, 20 nylon)—it's a more durable alternative for those who prefer knitting with wool.

Norwegian wool yarns:
- Fritidsgarn, woolen-spun yarn, 77 yd/70 m / 50 g, needles U. S. 9 / 5.5 mm.
- Peer Gynt, worsted-spun yarn, 98 yd/90 m / 50 g, needles U. S. 4-6 / 3.5-4 mm.
- Tove, wool yarn, 175 yd/160 m / 50 g, needles U. S. 4 / 3.5 mm.
- Tresko, sock yarn, 80% Norwegian wool, 20% nylon, 115 yd/105 m / 50 g, needles U. S. 2.5-4 / 3-3.5 mm.
- Tykk ull super bulky wool, 38 yd/35 m / 50 g, needles U. S. 15 / 10 mm (discontinued at the time of publishing).

Other Norwegian Spinning Mills

In the past, the textile industry was big business in Norway, but now there are only a few yarn producers left. At the same time, in the past few years, a few small mills that spin yarn with Norwegian wool have been established. Yarn such as 2-ply from Sjølingstad Uldvarefabrik, Symre from Telespinn, or Fin gammel from Selbu Spinneri can substitute for yarns such as Ask, Finull, or Tove.

Sjølingstad Uldvarefabrik was founded in 1894 outside Mandal and remained in business for 90 years. The mill produced worsted yarn fabrics, jacquard-woven blankets, and yarn. Today Sjølingstad is a living museum mill that shows how woolen goods were produced on old-style machines.
- 2-ply Sjølingstad yarn, woolen-spun yarn, 383 yd/350 m / 100 g.
- 3-ply Sjølingstad yarn, woolen-spun yarn, 251 yd/230 m / 100 g.

Telespinn is a farm-based mill in Flatdal in Telemark, and since its founding in 2008 has specialized in spinning mohair yarn and taking in fiber for commission spinning.
- Pan Sports, 70% Norwegian mohair, 30% Norwegian sheep's wool, 190 yd/174 m / 100 g, needles U. S. 4-8 / 3.5-5 mm.
- Symre knitting yarn, 2-ply, 80% Norwegian kid mohair, 20% Norwegian lamb's wool, 330 yd/302 m / 100 g, needles U. S. 1.5-6 / 2.5-4 mm.

Selbu Spinneri (Selbu Spinnery) in Klæbu in Trøndelag is a mini-mill established in 2010 to spin yarn from the traditional Norwegian spelsau sheep's wool. They take in wool from sheep owners who send it to them, and in return are sent yarn and other products, but the mill also spins its own yarns to sell. Their yarn is primarily natural colors and the production is small-scale.
- KRUS yarn (spun at Hillesvåg). The same grist as Ask from Hillesvåg, needles U. S. 1.5 / 2-2.5 mm
- Gimre, 2-ply yarn, several breed-specific versions available, 219 yd/200 m / 100 g, needles U. S. 2.5-4 / 3-3.5 mm
- Fin Gammel Selbu, 394 yd/360 m / 100 g, needles U. S. 0000-0 / 1-2 mm

1. Read through the entire pattern before you begin.
2. When a design is worked with several colors, it's very important to decide how to hold the individual strands. Here are some options:
   - Hold two strands over different fingers of the same hand (over the index finger and middle finger).
   - Hold both strands over the index finger and pick up the strands over or under each other as needed.
   - Hold two strands over the index fingers of your right hand and left hand.
   - Let the strand that isn't in use hang loosely, and change it each time you change colors.

   Try out each method and decide which you like best.
3. When you knit with two colors, make sure you don't pull the yarn in on the wrong side too hard or your piece will pucker.
4. We try to avoid floats that are too long between colors, but if you find the strands are too long on the wrong side, you can twist them around each other once on the wrong side, or wind them over and under each other as explained above.
5. Pullovers and cardigans in this book are a mix of unisex garments that can be worn by anyone, and patterns specifically designed to fit women or men; you should feel free to adapt them as desired. Be aware that a size S in a unisex sweater will be larger than size S in a women's sweater—check the garment's measurements before you begin knitting.
6. Gauge is very important for garment knitting in order to obtain the correct size and silhouette. The needle sizes listed in the patterns are only recommendations; you need to check your gauge by knitting a swatch. Measure 4 x 4 in / 10 x 10 cm on the swatch and count how many stitches/rows are within that area. If you have too many stitches, try larger needles; change to smaller needles if you have too few stitches. Gauge can change as you work, especially when knitting a single-color section of a patterned item or a part with small circumference—for example, a sleeve's gauge may come out differently than the body's.

ABBREVIATIONS and TERMS

BO	bind off (= UK cast off)	rep	repeat
CC	contrast (or pattern) color	rnd(s)	round(s)
ch	chain st	sc	single crochet (= UK double crochet)
cm	centimeters	sl m	slip marker
CO	cast on	ssk	[slip 1 knitwise] 2 times, knit the 2 sts
dpn	double-pointed needles		together through back loops (= 1 stitch
est	established = continue pattern as set		decreased; left-leaning decrease
in	inch(es)	st(s)	stitch(es)
k	knit	tbl	through back loop(s)
k2tog	knit 2 together = 1 stitch decreased; right-leaning decrease	tog	together
M1	make 1 = increase 1 stitch by picking up the strand	WS	wrong side
	between two stitches with the left needle tip,	yd	yards
	from front to back, and knit directly into back loop	yo	yarnover
MC	main (background) color	*–*	repeat the sequence between the asterisks
m	meter(s)	steek	A steek is a section of extra stitches added so
mm	millimeters		that you can knit in the round on a sweater body
p	purl		that will later be cut open for the two fronts of
pm	place marker		a cardigan or for the armholes from underarms
psso	pass slipped st over		to shoulders, or for the neck instructions for
RS	right side		working steek stitches and for reinforcing and
rem	remain(s) (ing)		cutting a steek are given in individual patterns.

Agat
WOMEN'S PULLOVER

Agat is both a trademark that was used by the Salhus factory in the 1930s and a semiprecious stone with bands of many colors. We thought the name was perfect for this pretty women's pullover in ochre or rust, with three harmonizing pattern colors.

This design with diamond shapes would have been produced in the latter half of the 1920s. At that time, it was knitted with beige heather or white as the main color and various contrast colors. The pattern was also knitted in red, white, and blue, and that variation inspired our new version in four colors.

Knitted samples from the 1920s and 30s.

DESIGN
Siv Dyvik

SKILL LEVEL
Experienced

SIZES
XXS-XS (S, M, L, XL, XXL)

FINISHED MEASUREMENTS
Chest: 31½ (35, 38½, 42¼, 45¾, 48¾) in /
80 (89, 98, 107, 116, 124) cm
Total Length: approx. 22 (22½, 22¾, 23¾, 24½, 25¼) in /
56 (57, 58, 60, 62, 64) cm
Sleeve Length: approx. 18¼ (18¼, 18½, 18½, 19, 19) in /
46 (46, 47, 47, 48, 48) cm or desired length

MATERIALS
Yarn:
CYCA #1 (fingering) Sandnes Garn Mini Alpakka
(100% alpaca, 164 yd/150 m / 50 g)

Yarn Colors and Amounts:
Suggestion 1
Color 1: Ochre 2035: 250 (300, 300, 350, 350, 400) g
Color 2: Natural 1012: 150 (150, 200, 200, 250, 250) g
Color 3: Dusty Green 7243: 50 (50, 50, 50, 50, 50) g
Color 4: Corn Yellow 2015: 50 (50, 50, 50, 50, 50) g

Suggestion 2
Color 1: Rust 3355: 250 (300, 300, 350, 350, 400) g
Color 2: Dusty Old Rose 4023: 150 (150, 200, 200, 250, 250) g
Color 3: Light Terracotta 3834: 50 (50, 50, 50, 50, 50) g
Color 4: Dusty Pistachio 9521: 50 (50, 50, 50, 50, 50) g

Needles:
U. S. sizes 1.5 and 2.5 / 2.5 and 3 mm:
circulars and sets of 5 dpn

GAUGE
27 sts in pattern = 4 in / 10 cm.
Adjust needle size to obtain correct gauge if necessary.

FRONT AND BACK
With Color 1 and smaller circular, CO 216 (240, 264, 288, 312, 336) sts. Join, being careful not to twist cast-on row; pm for beginning of rnd.
Work around in k1, p1 ribbing for 1¼ in / 3 cm.
Change to larger circular. Knit 1 rnd.
Continue in stockinette, following chart, until body is approx. 14¼ (14½, 15, 15½, 15¾, 16¼) in / 36 (37, 38, 39, 40, 41) cm long.
Now divide piece for front, back, and armholes: BO 8 sts and then:
k93 (105, 117, 129, 141, 153) = front; BO 15 sts = right underarm;
k93 (105, 117, 129, 141, 153) = back; BO 7 sts.
Set body aside while you knit the sleeves.

SLEEVES
With Color 1 and smaller dpn, CO 52 (54, 56, 58, 60, 62) sts. Divide sts onto dpn and join; pm for beginning of rnd.
Work around in k1, p1 ribbing for 1¼ in / 3 cm.
Change to larger dpn. Knit 1 rnd.
Continue in stockinette, following chart. Count out from arrow for center of sleeve to determine beginning of pattern for your size. Make sure pattern is centered on sleeve. **Note:** Always purl the center stitch of underarm.
Shape sleeve: Increase 1 st on each side of centered purl st approx. every ¾ (¾, ¾, ⅝, ⅝, ⅝) in / 2 (2, 2, 1.5, 1.5, 1.5) cm 18 (19, 20, 21, 22, 23) times = 88 (92, 96, 100, 104, 108) sts. Work new sts into pattern.
Continue in pattern until sleeve reaches specified or desired length.
End on the same pattern row as for front and back.
BO the center purl st + 7 sts on each side of it = 15 sts bound off for underarm and 73 (77, 81, 85, 89, 93) sts rem. Set sleeve aside and knit second sleeve the same way.

RAGLAN SHAPING

Arrange sleeves and body on larger circular in the following order and, *at the same time*, p2tog joining the first and last st of each piece = 4 sts decreased: back, first sleeve, front, second sleeve = total of 328 (360, 392, 424, 456, 488) sts.

Note: The purl decreases should be marked as the center of each raglan line and should always be purled.

Each marked st and the 2 sts before and after it should always be worked with Color 1.

Continue around following the chart over all the sts. Shape raglan on every other rnd by working k2tog after each marked st and ssk or k2tog tbl before each marked st = 8 sts decreased per round.

Decrease a total of 22 (23, 24, 25, 26, 27) times = 152 (176, 200, 224, 248, 272) sts rem.

BO the center front 21 (23, 25, 27, 29, 31) sts for front neck.

Knit to beginning of rnd and cut yarn.

Attach yarn at center front and work back and forth in stockinette and pattern.

Continue raglan shaping as before and, *at the same time*, BO at neck edge at beginning of each row 2, 2 (2,2; 2, 2, 2; 2, 2, 2; 2, 2, 2, 2; 2, 2, 2, 2, 2) sts and then 1 st until neck edge meets raglan shaping at each side.

Leave rem sts on needle.

NECKBAND

With Color 4 (Color Suggestion 1) or 2 (Color Suggestion 2) and smaller circular, pick up and knit approx. 14 sts per 2 in / 5 cm around neck.

Knit body sts on needle. Make sure total is a multiple of 2 sts (144 sts around neck for size M).

Work around in k1, p1 ribbing for approx. 1½ in / 4 cm.

BO loosely in ribbing.

Fold neckband in half and sew bound-off edge to WS.

FINISHING

Seam underarms. Weave in all ends neatly on WS.

Chart

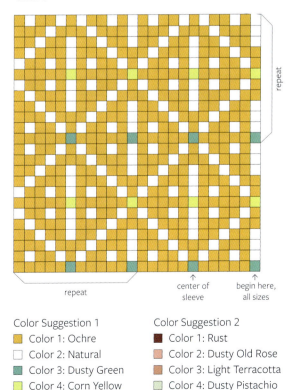

repeat

center of sleeve

begin here, all sizes

repeat

Color Suggestion 1	Color Suggestion 2
▨ Color 1: Ochre	▨ Color 1: Rust
☐ Color 2: Natural	▨ Color 2: Dusty Old Rose
▨ Color 3: Dusty Green	▨ Color 3: Light Terracotta
▨ Color 4: Corn Yellow	▨ Color 4: Dusty Pistachio

Safir

CARDIGAN

Taking brand names from the mineral world, including (Safir), was popular at Salhus in the 1930s. The pattern for this long jacket is from the same time period—it was probably in use between 1910 and 1930. This design also has a diamond motif and was knitted with white or gray/beige heather as the main color and pattern colors of black, yellow, green, or even pink. This new version, styled for everyone, has become a long cardigan with set-in sleeves. There are two color suggestions—one a little more colorful in light turquoise, and a classic one in gray and white.

The body is worked in the round with a steek, straight upward in pattern to the decreases shaping the neckline. The center front and armhole steeks are cut open in finishing. The sleeves are knitted straight in pattern and the stitch count increased as you work up. After a short facing is worked, they are bound off straight across when at the desired total length.

Knitted samples from the 1920s and '30s.

DESIGN
Kristin Wiola Ødegård

SKILL LEVEL
Experienced

SIZES
S (M, L, XL, XXL)

FINISHED MEASUREMENTS
Chest: 37¾ (41, 44, 47¼, 50¼) in /
96 (104, 112, 120, 128) cm
Total Length: 25¼ (27½, 28¾, 30½, 31) in /
64 (70, 73, 77, 79) cm
Sleeve Length: 18½ (18½, 19¼, 19¼, 19¾) in /
47 (47, 49, 49, 50) cm

MATERIALS
Yarn:
CYCA #2 (sport, baby) Hillesvåg Ask (100%
Norwegian wool, 344 yd/315 m / 100 g)
CYCA #3 (DK, light worsted) Hillesvåg Tinde pelsullgarn
(100% Norwegian pelt sheep wool, 284 yd/260 m / 100 g)

Yarn Colors and Amounts:
Suggestion 1
MC: Ask Light Green-Turquoise 316127: *Sport*
300 (350, 400, 450, 450) g
CC: Tinde Light Turquoise 652130: *DK*
100 (100, 150, 150, 200) g

Suggestion 2
MC: Ask Natural White 316057: 300 (350, 400, 450, 450) g
CC: Tinde Natural Gray 652115: 100 (100, 150, 150, 200) g

Notions:
12-16 buttons, ⅝ in / 18 mm in diameter
Ribbon, 54¼-59 in / 130-150 cm long, to cover cut edges

Needles:
U. S. sizes 2.5 and 4 / 3 and 3.5 mm: circulars
32 in / 80 cm and sets of 5 dpn; + 16 in /
40 cm circular, U. S. size 4 / 3.5 mm

GAUGE
25 sts x 27 rnds in pattern on larger
needles = 4 x 4 in / 10 x 10 cm.
Adjust needle size to obtain correct gauge if necessary.

FRONT AND BACK
With MC and smaller circular, CO 241 (261, 281,
301, 321) sts. Work back and forth in k1, p1
ribbing for 1½ (1½, 2, 2, 2) in / 4 (4, 5, 5, 5) cm.
Change to larger circular and CO 7 new sts (steek)
at beginning of next row.
Join and work around in pattern following chart.
When body measures 1½ (1½, 2, 2, 2) in / 4 (4, 5, 5,
5) cm less than total length, BO the center front
27 (29, 29, 31, 31) sts, including steek sts, for
the neck.
Now work back and forth in pattern, and, *at the
same time*, decrease to shape neckline at the
beginning of each row: BO 2, 2, 1, 1, 1, 1 sts =
total of 8 sts decreased at each side for all sizes.
Continue working back and forth in pattern until
body measures 25¼ (27½, 28¾, 30½, 31) in / 64
(70, 73, 77, 79) cm.
Finish with a whole or half pattern repeat. BO rem
sts loosely.

SLEEVES
With MC and smaller dpn, CO 50 (54, 54, 56, 58)
sts. Divide sts onto dpn and join. Work back and
forth in k1, p1 ribbing for 1½ (1½, 2, 2, 2) in / 4
(4, 5, 5, 5) cm.
Change to larger dpn. Knit 1 rnd, increasing 8 sts
evenly spaced round = 58 (62, 62, 64, 66) sts.
Note: Always purl last st of rnd to indicate center of
the underarm and center of sleeve shaping.
Count out from arrow for center of sleeve to
determine starting st for your size. Make sure
pattern is centered on sleeve.
Increase 1 st on each side of centered purl st of
underarm every ¾ (¾, ⅝, ⅝, ⅝) in / 2 (2, 1.5,
1.5, 1.5) cm until there are 90 (100, 110, 120,
120) sts total. Work new sts into pattern.

Color Suggestion 2

When sleeve is approx. 18½ (18½, 19¼, 19¼, 19¾) in / 47 (47, 49, 49, 50) cm long, end with a whole or half pattern repeat. Turn sleeve wrong side out and knit ¾ in / 2 cm in stockinette for a facing. BO all sts loosely.

Set sleeve aside while you knit the second sleeve the same way.

FINISHING

Mark the sides of the body where the sleeves will be sewn in. Measure across top of sleeve to determine armhole depth.

Machine-stitch 2 zigzag lines on each side of center st of each armhole and center front steek.

Carefully cut steeks open up center stitch.

Join shoulders.

Sew in sleeves by hand. Fold facing over cut steek edges and loosely sew down.

NECKBAND

With MC and smaller circular, pick up and knit 4 sts for every 5 sts around neck edge for a total of 91-101 sts.

It is important that the stitch count be a multiple of 2 + 1 sts so that the first and last sts will be the same.

Work back and forth in k1, p1 ribbing for 1¼ (1¼, 1½, 1½, 1½) in / (3 (3, 4, 4, 4) cm.

BO knitwise on WS.

BUTTONHOLES

Space buttonholes on a front band about 2 in / 5 cm apart.

Make a buttonhole by binding off 2 sts and then casting on 2 sts over the gap on the next row.

BUTTONHOLE/BUTTON BANDS

For women's sweater, buttonholes on are usually placed right front band.

For men's sweater, buttonholes are usually placed on left front band.

RIGHT FRONT BAND

With MC and smaller circular, pick up and knit 3 sts for every 4 rows along right front edge and neckband.

Knit the first row on WS.

Men's: Work back and forth in k1, p1 ribbing for 1¼ (1¼, 1½, 1½, 1½) in / (3 (3, 4, 4, 4) cm.

Women's: Work back and forth in k1, p1 ribbing for ⅝ (⅝, ¾, ¾ ¾) in / 1.5 (1.5, 2, 2, 2) cm.

Make a buttonhole (see Buttonholes on previous page) every 2 in / 5 cm along the band.

After buttonholes, work in k1, p1 ribbing for ⅝ (⅝, ¾, ¾ ¾) in / 1.5 (1.5, 2, 2, 2) cm.

Men's and Women's: BO knitwise on WS.

LEFT FRONT BAND

With MC and smaller circular, pick up and knit 3 sts for every 4 rows along left front edge and neckband.

Knit the first row on WS.

Women's: Work back and forth in k1, p1 ribbing for 1¼ (1¼, 1½, 1½, 1½) in / (3 (3, 4, 4, 4) cm.

Men's: Work back and forth in k1, p1 ribbing for ⅝ (⅝, ¾, ¾ ¾) in / 1.5 (1.5, 2, 2, 2) cm.

Make a buttonhole (see Buttonholes on previous page) every 2 in / 5 cm along the band.

After buttonholes, work in k1, p1 ribbing for ⅝ (⅝, ¾, ¾ ¾) in / 1.5 (1.5, 2, 2, 2) cm.

Women's and Men's: BO knitwise on WS.

Sew on buttons (with MC yarn). Weave in all ends neatly on WS.

Hand-sew on ribbon on WS to cover cut edges.

Chart

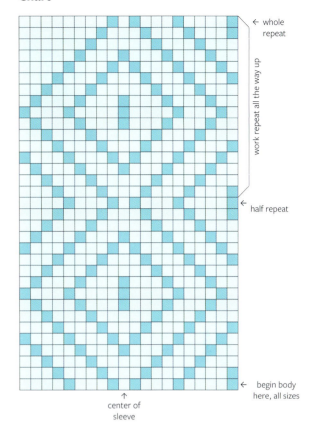

← whole repeat

work repeat all the way up

← half repeat

← begin body here, all sizes

↑ center of sleeve

☐ MC
🟦 CC

Hedvig

WOMEN'S CARDIGAN

This motif is from the period 1910-1920. As with many of the patterns from that time, it was knitted with white or a heather yarn for the main color and sometimes very intense contrast colors.

This long women's cardigan has set-in sleeves and a slight A-line silhouette, with attractive contrast stripes in. The rest of the sweater is gray and white and is simple and sweet, with neat details. The jacket is named for Hedvig Tellevik, who worked as a seamstress at Salhus Tricotagefabrik for 33 years.

Knitted samples from the period between 1910 and 1920.

Hedvig has been a long-time member of the Friends of the Museum Association, always eager to share her sewing skills.

DESIGN
Berit Løkken, Hillesvåg Ullvarefabrikk

SKILL LEVEL
Experienced

SIZES
S (M, L, XL, XXL)

FINISHED MEASUREMENTS
Chest: 35½ (36¾, 39½, 40½, 43¼) in /
90 (93, 100, 103, 110) cm
Total Length: 28¾ (29½, 30¼, 31, 32) in /
73 (75, 77, 79, 81) cm
Sleeve Length: 19¼ (19¾, 20, 20½, 21) in /
49 (50, 51, 52, 53) cm

MATERIALS
Yarn:
CYCA #2 (sport, baby) Hillesvåg Ask (100%
Norwegian wool, 344 yd/315 m / 100 g)

Yarn Colors and Amounts:
MC: Dark Gray Heather 316061: 400 (450, 500, 550, 600) g
CC1: Natural White 316057: 200 (200, 250, 250, 250) g
CC2: Brass Yellow 316092: 50 (50, 50, 100, 100) g

Notions:
4 buttons

Needles:
U. S. size 1.5 / 2.5 mm: circulars 16 and
32 in / 40 and 80 cm; set of 5 dpn
U. S. sizes 2.5 and 4 / 3 and 3.5 mm: circulars
16 and 32 in / 40 and 80 cm; sets of 5 dpn

GAUGE
24 sts x 32 rnds in stockinette pattern on U. S.
4 / 3.5 mm needles = 4 x 4 in / 10 x 10 cm.
Adjust needle size to obtain correct gauge if necessary.

BODY

With CC2 and U. S. 1.5 / 2.5 mm circular, CO 257 (265, 281, 289, 305) sts. Work 4 rows back and forth in stockinette (the first row = WS and is purled), knit 1 row on WS (foldline), and then work 4 more rows stockinette.

Fold the facing in and join to live sts: *k2tog joining 1 live st and 1 cast-on row stitch*; rep * to * across.

If you prefer, you can sew the facing down instead.

With CC2, knit 1 row. CO 5 new sts at center front for steek (steek sts are not worked in pattern and will later be cut open; work steek sts as p1, k3, p1 for easier finishing).

Change to U. S. 4 / 3.5 mm circular and join to work in the round, Knit 2 rnds with MC.

Continue in the round with pattern following Chart 1. Repeat Chart 1 a total of 3 times in length and then work from Chart 2 to finished length.

Begin as indicated on the chart and repeat pattern around.

Pm at each side. Measure when body is approx. 4 (4, 4¼, 4¼, 4¾) in / 10 (10 11, 11, 12) cm above foldline. Each front has 64 (66, 70, 72, 76) sts (+ steek sts) and back has 129 (133, 141, 145, 153) sts.

Shape each side as follows: Knit until 2 sts before marker, ssk, sl m, k2tog; rep at next marker = 4 sts decreased around.

Rep this decrease rnd every 1¼ in / 3 cm a total of 12 times = 209 (217, 233, 241, 257) sts rem.

Now continue in pattern without decreasing.

When body is approx. 2¾ in / 7 cm shorter than total length = approx. 26 (26¾, 27½, 28¼, 29¼) in / 66 (68, 70, 72, 74) cm, BO the center 14 (16, 18, 20, 22) sts for front neck (+ steek sts).

Instead, if you prefer, you can BO the 5 steek sts and place the rest of the sts on a stitch holder.

Continue, working back and forth. At neck edge, on every other row, BO 4, 3, 2, 1 sts or place those sts on a holder = 34 (36, 38, 40, 42) sts for front neck + steek sts).

When body is approx. ¾ in / 2 cm less than total
length, BO center 25 (27, 29, 31, 33) sts of back
for back neck (or place the sts on a holder).
Work each side separately.

At neck edge, on every other row, BO 3, 2 sts.
Continue in pattern to full length.

With CC2, knit 1 row before binding off. BO with
CC2.

Work other side of back to correspond.

SLEEVES

With MC and U. S. 1.5 / 2.5 mm dpn, CO 57 (59, 61,
63, 63) sts. Divide sts onto dpn and join to work
in the round.

Knit 4 rnds and then purl 1 rnd on RS (foldline) and
then knit 4 more rnds.

Change to U. S. 2.5 / 3 mm dpn and CC2. Knit 1 rnd,
purl 4 rnds, knit 1 rnd.

With MC, knit 4 rnds and, *at the same time*, on the
4th rnd, increase 4 sts evenly spaced around.

Change to U. S. 4 / 3.5 mm dpn and work in pattern
following Chart 3.

On the chart, the center of the sleeve is marked with
*. Count out from center to determine beginning
st for your size. Make sure pattern is centered on
sleeve.

At the same time, on every 6th rnd, increase 2 sts at
center of underarm until there are 101 (103,
105, 107, 109) sts.

After completing charted rows, change to U. S. 2.5
/ 3 mm dpn or short circular and continue in
stockinette with MC.

When sleeve measures 19¼ (19¾, 20, 20½, 21) in
/ 49 (50, 51, 52, 53) cm from foldline, knit 3
rnds with CC2 and then change to U. S. 1.5 / 2.5
mm needle. Turn sleeve wrong side out and knit
around for 1 in / 2.5 cm for facing. BO loosely.

Make the second sleeve the same way.

FINISHING

Gently steam press pieces on wrong side under a
damp pressing cloth.

Measure top of sleeve width and mark depth of
armhole to same measurement.

Machine-stitch 2 zigzag lines on each side of center
st of each armhole and center front steek.

Carefully cut steek and armholes open up center
stitch.

Join shoulders.

With U. S. 1.5 / 2.5 mm circular and MC, pick up and
knit approx. 125 (129, 131, 133, 135) sts around
neck. Work back and forth with MC.

Purl 1 row on WS and then work 10 rows k1, p1
ribbing.

Knit 1 row with CC2 and then purl 1 row on RS
(foldline). Work 12 rows in stockinette,
decreasing 6 sts evenly spaced across on first
row.

BO.

Fold neck facing in half and sew down smoothly on
WS.

If you didn't join the lower edge facing to body
previously, sew it down.

FRONT BANDS

Left front band: With U. S. 1.5 / 2.5 mm circular and
MC, pick up and knit approx. 3 sts for every 4
rows along left front (button band).

Work back and forth in k1, p1 ribbing for 1¼ in / 3
cm.

BO in ribbing.

Right front band: Work as for left front band until
band measures approx. ⅝ in / 1.5 cm.

Make 4 buttonholes, with top one on neckband and
the rest spaced about 3¼ in / 8 cm apart.

Buttonhole: BO 2 sts. On the next row, CO 2 sts
over gap.

Continue in ribbing until band is 1¼ in / 3 cm wide. BO in ribbing.

To cover the cut edges, you can sew on ribbon or knit a facing as follows: Pick up and knit sts along back of each front band (but not on neckband or lower edge). Work back and forth in stockinette for approx. ⅝ in / 1.5 cm. BO and sew down facing on WS.

Fold facing on each sleeve at foldline and sew down facing on WS.

Attach sleeves by hand. Fold facing over cut steek edges and loosely sew down.

Sew on buttons. Weave in all ends neatly on WS.

FINISHING

Lay cardigan on a damp towel and pat out to finished measurements. Leave until completely dry. Alternatively, soak cardigan in lukewarm water, spin out in a spin dryer (centrifuge), and pat it out to dry on flat surface.

Chart 1

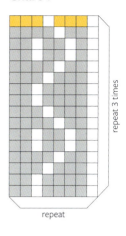

repeat 3 times

repeat

Chart 3

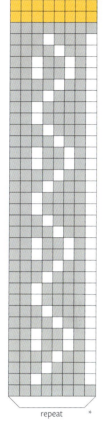

repeat   *

Chart 2

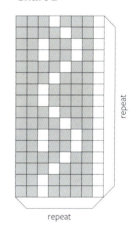

repeat

repeat

☐ MC
☐ CC1
🟨 CC2
*   Center of sleeve

We've used the motif from the Hedvig cardigan for a pillow cover, which is closer in color to the original sample in the archives: dark gray, white, and rose heather. The cover is knitted in the round, seamed at the top, and closed at the bottom edge with smart crocheted buttons in a contrast color. Hedvig was a seamstress at the Salhus Tricotagefabrik and we believe she would have liked to have this pillow on her sofa.

Knitted samples from the period between 1910 and 1920.

DESIGN
Norsk Trikotasjemuseum (Norwegian Knitting Industry Museum)

SKILL LEVEL
Experienced

FINISHED MEASUREMENTS
17¾ x 17¾ in / 45 x 45 cm

MATERIALS
Yarn:
CYCA #2 (sport, baby) Hillesvåg Ask (100% Norwegian wool, 344 yd/315 m / 100 g)

Yarn Colors and Amounts:
MC: Dark Gray Heather 316061: 100 g
CC1: Bleached White 316047: 100 g
CC2: Deep Rose Heather 316568: 50 g

Notions:
Pillow insert, 17¾ x 17¾ in / 45 x 45 cm; 13 small buttons if you don't want to make fastenings yourself

Needles:
U. S. size 2.5 / 3 mm: circular 24 in / 60 cm

Crochet Hook:
U. S. size D-3 / 3 mm

GAUGE
24 sts x 32 rnds in stockinette pattern
= 4 x 4 in / 10 x 10 cm.
Adjust needle size to obtain correct gauge if necessary.

Chart

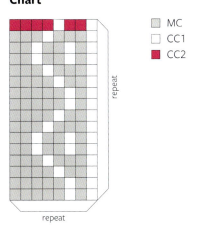

☐ MC
☐ CC1
■ CC2

repeat

repeat

PILLOW COVER

With MC and circular, CO 200 sts (the pattern repeat is a multiple of 25 sts). Join, being careful not to twist cast-on row; pm for beginning of rnd. Work around in pattern following chart until piece is approx. 17¾ in / 45 cm long.

We finished on the chart row just below the rose stripe.

BO and seam the top with MC.

Seam lower edge 1½ in / 4 cm in from each side towards the center.

Crochet a round of sc all around the opening.

Work a row of sc on one side (front) and make buttonholes as follows: 4 sc, *ch 2, skip 2 sts on previous row, work 5 sc*.

Rep * to * until there are about 13 buttonholes.

End with sc up to sewn edge on opposite corner (approx. 4 sc). Cut yarn and fasten off.

Weave in all ends neatly on WS.

BUTTONS

Sew purchased buttons on the back or make them yourself:

Begin with a yarn end about 4 in / 10 cm long.

Ch 4, join into a ring with 1 sl st into 1st ch. Work 1 rnd of sc, increasing to about 8 sts.

Bring yarn through, leaving a 4 in / 10 cm yarn end.

Sew this end back and forth several times on the back so that it forms a small, firm button; cut yarn.

Use the other yarn end to sew the button securely to the back of the pillow cover.

Make a button for every buttonhole. The buttons should be of sufficient size to pass through the buttonhole on the front. It can be a little tricky to button the cover together, but the front and back will look nicer if they are closed tightly together. We used 13 buttons and buttonholes, but you can make more or fewer.

Finish by gently steam pressing cover into final shape/size under a damp pressing cloth.

Oline DRESS

This pattern motif was first used around 1920 before it reappeared on wool sweaters in the late 1960s. It's reminiscent of other classic "Icelander" patterns with diagonal elements, but the addition of horizontal stripes gives it a different look. Here it decorates the yoke and sleeve tops on an elegant dress in burgundy. The dress was named after Oline Havre (1877-1962), who worked at the Salhus factory—together with her husband, knitter Nikolai Knudsen (1884-1962).[13]

The dress is knitted with a straight silhouette which suits most body shapes. The ribbing at the bottom edge draws in the piece while allowing more room for the hips.

Knitted samples from 1910 and 1967-68.

DESIGN
Siv Dyvik

SKILL LEVEL
Experienced

SIZES
XS (S, M, L, XL)

FINISHED MEASUREMENTS
Chest: 35½ (37¾, 40¼, 43, 45¼) in /
90 (96, 102, 109, 115) cm
Total Length: approx. 32¼ (33, 34, 34¾, 35½) in /
82 (84, 86, 88, 90) cm
Sleeve Length: approx. 18¼ (18¼, 18½, 18½, 19) in /
46 (46, 47, 47, 48) cm or desired length

MATERIALS
Yarn:
CYCA #2 (sport, baby) Rauma Finull PT2 (100%
Norwegian wool, 191 yd/175 m / 50 g)

Yarn Colors and Amounts:
Suggestion 1
Color 1: Dark Burgundy 488: 450 (500, 500, 550, 600) g
Color 2: Powder Rose 4087: 50 (50, 50, 50, 50) g
Color 3: Burgundy 497: 50 (50, 50, 50, 50) g

Suggestion 2
Color 1: Gray 404: 450 (500, 500, 550, 600) g
Color 2: Burgundy 497: 50 (50, 50, 50, 50) g
Color 3: Powder Rose 4087: 50 (50, 50, 50, 50) g

Needles:
U. S. sizes 1.5 and 2.5 / 2.5 and 3 mm: circulars
32 or 40 in / 80 or 100 cm; set of 5 dpn; shorter
circular of smaller size for neckband

GAUGE
25 sts in stockinette on larger needles = 4 in / 10 cm.
Adjust needle size to obtain correct gauge if necessary.

FRONT AND BACK
With Color 1 and smaller circular, CO 224 (240,
256, 272, 288) sts. Join, being careful not to
twist cast-on row; pm for beginning of rnd. Work
around as follows:
Rnd 1: (K1, p1) around.
Rnd 2: Knit.
Rep Rnds 1-2 until piece measures 1¼ in / 3 cm.
Change to larger circular and pm at each side with
112 (120, 128, 136, 144) sts each for front and
back.
Continue around in stockinette until body measures
24½ (24¾, 25¼, 25½, 26) in / 62 (63, 64, 65,
66) cm (or desired length to underarm).
Divide body as follows:
BO the 1st 6 sts;
k100 (108, 116, 124, 132) = front;
BO 12 sts—right underarm;
k100 (108, 116, 124, 132) = back;
BO rem 6 sts.
Set body aside while you knit the sleeves.

SLEEVES
With Color 1 and smaller dpn, CO 46 (48, 50, 52,
54) sts. Divide sts onto dpn and join; pm for
beginning of rnd. Work around as follows:
Rnd 1: (K1, p1) around.
Rnd 2: Knit.
Rep Rnds 1-2 until piece measures 1¼ in / 3 cm.
Change to larger dpn and knit 1 rnd, increasing
evenly spaced around to 50 (52, 54, 56, 58) sts
Continue around in stockinette, following the chart.
Work Chart 3 times in length and then continue
with Color 1 only.
At the same time, increase 2 sts centered on
underarm approx. every ¾ (¾, ¾, ⅝, ⅝) in / 2
(2, 2, 2, 1.5, 1.5) cm 19 (20, 21, 22, 23) times =
88 (92, 96, 100, 104) sts.
Continue in stockinette until sleeve is desired length
to underarm.

BO 12 sts centered on underarm = 76 (80, 84, 88, 92) sts rem.

Set sleeve aside while you knit second sleeve the same way.

RAGLAN SHAPING

Arrange all the pieces on larger circular as follows:

Back, first sleeve, front, second sleeve = a total of 352 (376, 400, 424, 448) sts.

Pm at each intersection of body and sleeve = 4 markers. The rnd begins at a join on the back.

Knit 2 rnds following the chart over all the sts without decreasing. (Rep pattern 6 times in length and then work the rest of the dress with Color 1 only).

At the same time, on the 3rd rnd, begin decreasing for raglan as follows:

K2tog after each marker and k2tog tbl (or ssk) before each marker = 8 sts decreased per rnd.
Note: The pattern won't always align at raglan decrease lines.

Decrease as above on every other rnd until you've worked 26 (28, 30, 32, 34) decrease rnds and 144 (152, 160, 168, 176) sts rem.

NECKBAND

Slip rem sts to smaller circular. Or, if you prefer, keep sts on larger circular and decrease a few sts on 1st rnd so neckband won't be too wide.

Continue with Color 1 and work around as follows:

Rnd 1: (K1, p1) around.

Rnd 2: Knit.

Rep Rnds 1-2 until piece measures 1¼ in / 3 cm. ending with Rnd 1.

BO loosely knitwise.

Seam underarms.

Weave in all ends neatly on WS.

Chart

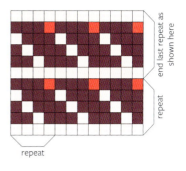

end last repeat as shown here

repeat

repeat

■ Color 1
□ Color 2
■ Color 3

Color Suggestion 2

Oline

The "Icelander" sweater called Hekla, from the Salhus Tricotage-fabrik, had a classic pattern with diagonal pattern stitches and was made from the 1940s onward. Another motif combined diagonal pattern stitches with horizontal lines. These pillows play with variations of these two patterns, knitted in four different color combinations. The covers fit over pillows 17¾ x 17¾ in / 45 x 45 cm or slightly larger. The button closures along the bottom edge are both decorative and practical, especially when you need to wash the covers.

The blue and white, green and white, and yellow pillows are knitted with Tinde pelsull (pelt wool) and Sol lamb's-wool yarns from Hillesvåg. The light brown and white pillow cover with multi-color dots is knitted with Museumstvinn, a worsted-spun yarn from the Norwegian Knitting Industry Museum.

Knitted samples from the 1910s (top) and 1958.

DESIGN

Siri Angela Gamborg, Norwegian Knitting Industry Museum

SKILL LEVEL

Experienced

FINISHED MEASUREMENTS

17¾ x 17¾ in / 45 x 45 cm

MATERIALS

Yarn:

CYCA #2 (sport, baby) Hillesvåg Sol Lamullgarn (100% Norwegian lamb's wool, 317 yd/290 m / 100 g)

CYCA #3 (DK, light worsted) Hillesvåg Tinde Pelsullgarn (100% Norwegian wool, 284 yd/260 m / 100 g)

Yarn Colors and Amounts:

Pillow Cover 1 (blue):

MC: Tinde Petroleum 652105: 100 g
CC1: Tinde Medium Blue 652135: 100 g
CC2: Tinde Light Denim Blue 652113: 50 g
CC3: Sol White 58400: 100 g
CC4: Tinde Turquoise 652106: 100 g

Pillow Cover 2 (green and white):

MC: Tinde Lime 652107: 100 g
CC1: Tinde Grass Green 652134: 100 g
CC2: Sol White 58400: 100 g

Pillow Cover 3 (yellow):

MC: Tinde Cognac 652103: 100 g
CC1: Tinde Ochre 652108: 100 g
CC2: Tinde Natural Grey 652115: 100 g

Notions:

Pillow insert, 17¾ x 17¾ in / 45 x 45 cm
8 small buttons, if you don't want to make fastenings yourself

Needles:

U. S. size 2.5-6 / 3-4 mm: circular 24 in / 60 cm

Crochet Hook:

U. S. size D-3 / 3 mm

GAUGE

22 sts in stockinette pattern = 4 in / 10 cm.
Adjust needle size to obtain correct gauge if necessary.

PILLOW COVER

With MC and circular, CO 100 sts for the back. Work 4 rows back and forth in stockinette.

CO 100 sts for the front and join with back to work in the round.

Pm for beginning of rnd and between front and back.

Knit 2 rnds. The back will be longer than the front and will also have buttonholes.

BUTTONHOLES

K11, yo, k2tog, k7, yo, k2tog, k8, yo, k2tog, k7, yo, k2tog, 8, yo, k2tog, k7, yo, k2tog, k8, yo, k2tog, k7, yo, k2tog, k11.

On next rnd, knit each yarnover.

Knit 1 rnd with MC.

Work following pattern chart once in length.

FINISHING

On Rnd 136, BO all sts.

Method 1: Bind off as usual and seam cover along top edge.

Method 2: Place all the sts on one needle, alternating one from front and one from back. BO as usual, working with pairs of sts.

Weave in all ends neatly on WS.

BUTTONS

Buy 8 small buttons or make 8 small crocheted
   buttons with your choice of color:
   Ch 5, join into a ring with 1 sl st into 1st ch. Work
   2 sc, ch 2, 2 sc around center hole. Work 5 sc on
   next rnd; draw out the yarn and pull it through
   the "hole" in the center. The button will roll
   inwards but you can pull it outwards with your
   fingers so it will lie flatter.
   Ball buttons: Work 4 sc in the first ring of sc and
   then 3 on the next rnd so that button rolls into a
   little ball. Using a darning needle, sew a bit up and
   down to firm up the ball and make it completely
   round.
Overlap the front with the buttonholes over the back
   and sew the buttons securely to the back, making
   sure that they fit into the buttonholes.
Finish by gently steam pressing cover into final shape/
   size under a damp pressing cloth.

Chart,
Pillow Cover 1

- ■ **MC:** Petroleum
- ■ **CC1:** Medium Blue
- ▦ **CC2:** Light Denim Blue
- □ **CC3:** Sol White
- ▨ **CC4:** Turquoise

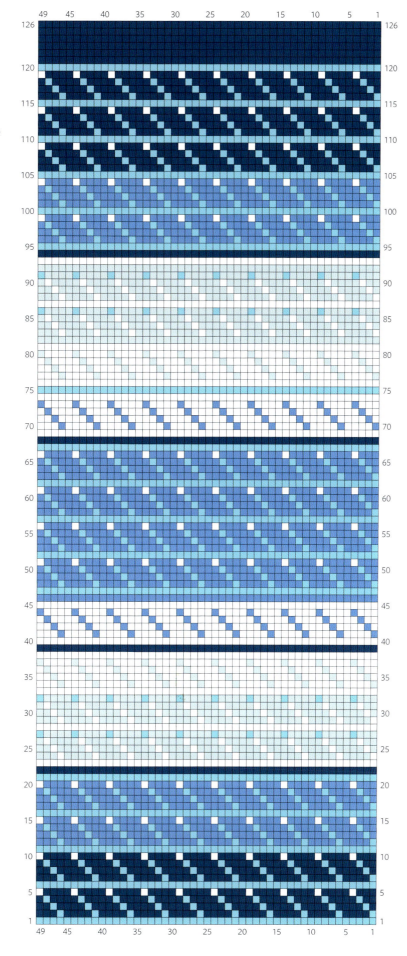

**Chart,
Pillow Cover 2**

■ **MC:** Lime
■ **CC1:** Grass Green
□ **CC2:** White

**Chart,
Pillow Cover 3**

■ **MC:** Cognac
■ **CC1:** Ochre
□ **CC2:** Natural
    Gray

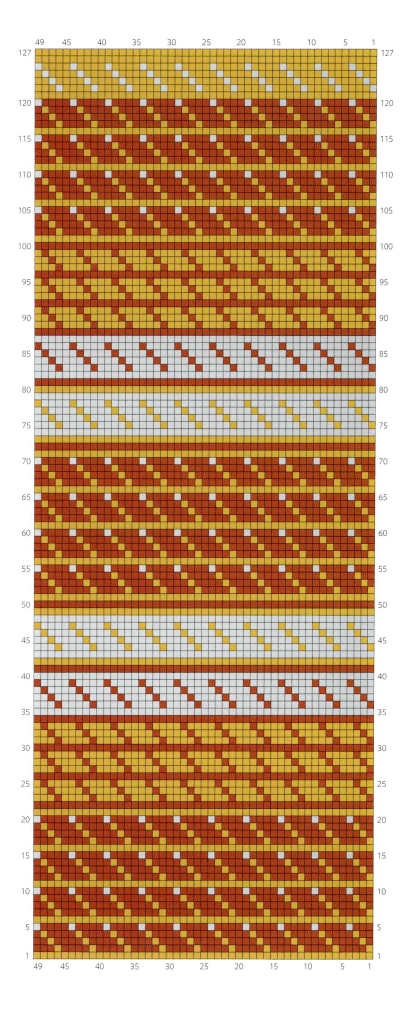

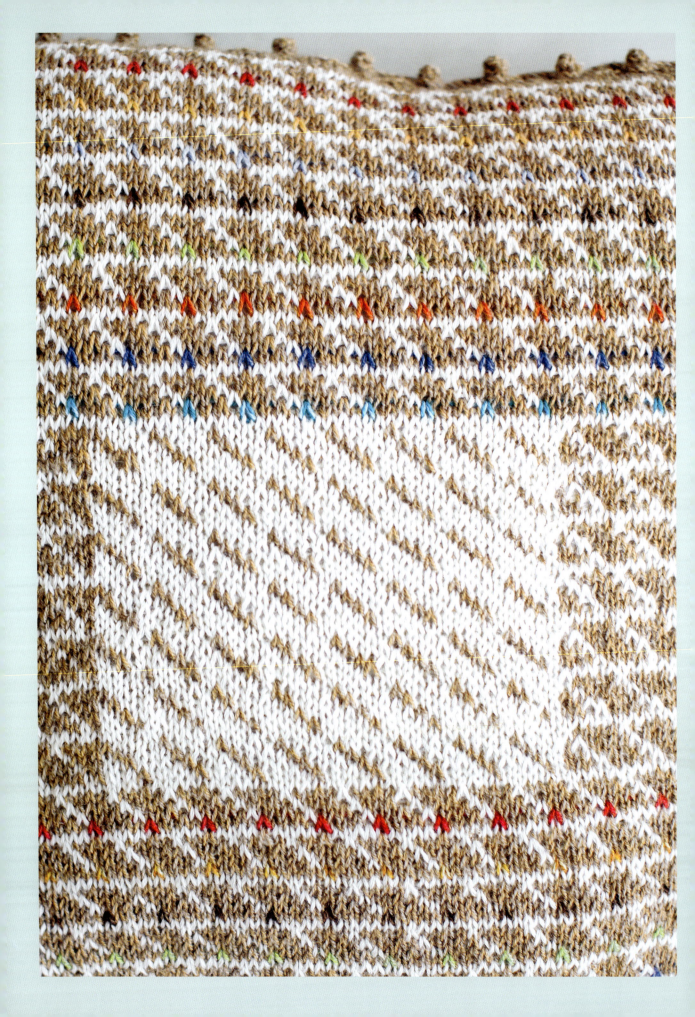

Oline

REMNANT YARN COVER

DESIGN

Siri Angela Gamborg, Norwegian Knitting Industry Museum

SKILL LEVEL

Experienced

FINISHED MEASUREMENTS

17¾ x 17¾ in / 45 x 45 cm

MATERIALS

Yarn:

CYCA #3 (DK, light worsted) Norwegian Knitting Industry Museum Museumstvinn (100% wool, 295 yd/270 m / 100 g)

Yarn Colors and Amounts:

MC: Light Brown Heather (Krumler) 100-120 g

CC: Natural White: 100 g

Assorted colors, approx. 14-20, about 47¼ in / 120 cm of each

Notions:

Pillow insert, 17¾ x 17¾ in / 45 x 45 cm

8 small buttons, if you don't want to make fastenings yourself

Needles:

U. S. size 4-6 / 3.5-4 mm: 24 in / 60 cm

Crochet Hook:

U. S. size A / 2 mm

GAUGE

21 sts in stockinette pattern = 4 in / 10 cm.

Adjust needle size to obtain correct gauge if necessary.

PILLOW COVER

With MC and circular, CO 200 sts. Join, being careful not to twist cast-on row; pm for beginning of rnd. Work 1 rnd k1, p1 ribbing. Now work in pattern following chart. **Note:** The chart only shows half of one side.

On the last rnd, BO with one of the following methods:

Method 1: Bind off as usual and seam cover along top edge.

Method 2: Place all the sts on one needle, alternating one from front and one from back. BO as usual, working with pairs of sts.

Weave in all ends neatly on WS.

BUTTONHOLES and BALL BUTTONS

Buy 8 small buttons or make 8 small crocheted buttons with your choice of color.

With crochet hook, work sc all around the cover edges and then make buttonholes along the front: Beginning at corner of side to be buttoned, work 11 sc and then ch 3, *5 sc, ch 3*; rep * to * along edge until you've made 8 buttonholes, ending with 11 sc to corner.

Make 8 small crocheted ball buttons in color(s) of your choice:

Ch 5, join into a ring with 1 sl st into 1st ch. Work 2 sc, ch 2, 2 sc around center hole. Work 4 sc on next rnd and then 3 sc on following rnd so that the button rolls in to a little ball. Using a darning needle, sew a bit up and down to firm up the ball and make it completely round.

Sew the buttons securely to edge of cover back. Seam the front and back at the corners on each side up from corner to first/last buttonhole.

Finish by gently steam pressing cover into final shape/size under a damp pressing cloth.

Chart

■ Light Brown
  Heather
  (Krumler)
□ Natural White
◩ Assorted colors

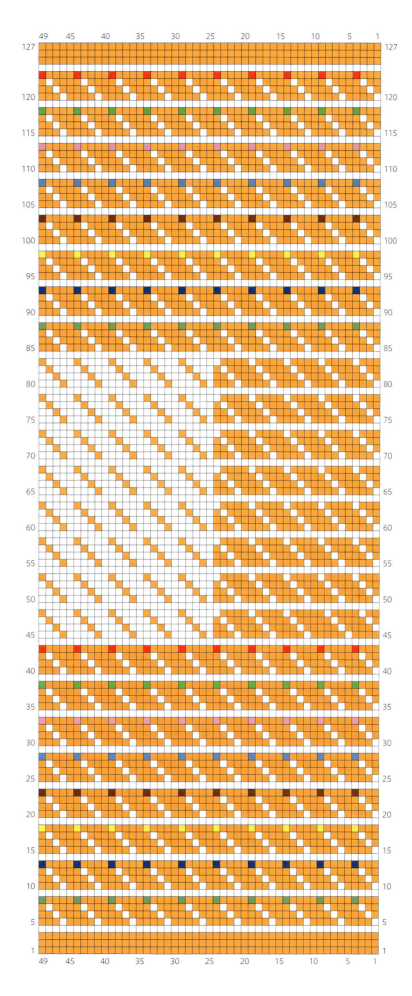

Clausen

MEN'S CARDIGAN

The motif for this sweater is relatively recent, and was used for wool sweaters in the late 1970s and early 1980s. Many different combinations of three colors appeared in this motif, which may remind you of horseshoes, crosses, or zeros. Perhaps the motif is a distant relative of the OXO designs from the Shetland Fair Isle tradition? We liked the pattern best in two colors, for a more subtle look. It can also be knitted with one strongly contrasting main color and two different tones of the same contrast color for a tone-on-tone effect. Here, it has served as inspiration for this men's cardigan with raglan sleeves, a shawl collar, and colors reminiscent of the 1970s. The sweater was named for the first Clausen at Salhus, the factory's founder, Phillip Christian Clausen (1837-1909).

The factory's founder, Phillip Christian Clausen.

Knitted samples from 1970s-80s.

DESIGN
Birger Berge

SKILL LEVEL
Experienced

SIZES
S (M, L, XL, XXL)

FINISHED MEASUREMENTS
Chest: 35½ (39½, 43¼, 47¼, 51¼) in /
90 (100, 110, 120, 130) cm
Sleeve Length: 22½ (23¼, 23¼, 23¾, 23¾) in /
57 (59, 59, 60, 60) cm

MATERIALS
Yarn:
CYCA #5 (bulky, chunky, craft, rug) Hillesvåg Troll
(100% Norwegian wool, 125 yd/114 m / 100 g)

Yarn Colors and Amounts:
Color 1: Charcoal Gray 02733: 500 (550, 550, 600, 600) g
Color 2: Steel Gray 02741: 400 (450, 450, 500, 500) g
Color 3: Ochre 02713: 200 (200, 200, 250, 250) g

Notions:
8 buttons

Needles:
U. S. size 9-10 / 5.5-6 mm: circulars 32 or
40 in / 80 or 100 cm; set of 5 dpn
U. S. size 8 / 5 mm: circular 32 in / 80 cm; set of
5 dpn for shawl collar and ribbed bands

GAUGE
14 sts in stockinette pattern on larger
needles = 4 in / 10 cm.
Adjust needle size to obtain correct gauge if necessary.

BODY

With Ochre and smaller circular, CO 127 (142, 155, 171, 185) sts. Work 10 rows back and forth in k2, p2 ribbing.

Change to larger circular. CO 5 sts at center front for steek (extra sts to be cut open for center front; steek sts not included in st counts) and join. Knit 1 rnd, increasing 1 st at center back.

Continue, working charted pattern in the round, with sts divided as follows:
Front: 31 (35, 38, 42, 45) sts beginning at X on chart.
Purl 1 st.
Back: 63 (71, 79, 85, 93) sts; center back = X on chart.
Purl 1 st.
Front: 31 (35, 38, 42, 45) sts.

Continue as est until body measures 17¼ (17¾, 18¼, 18½, 19¾) in / 44 (45, 46, 47, 50) cm from cast-on row. Now BO 4 sts on each side of each purl st, and, at the same time, BO each purl st.
Set body aside while you knit sleeves.

SLEEVES

With Ochre and smaller dpn, CO 28 (32, 32, 36, 36) sts. Divide sts onto dpn and join. Work 8 rnds in k2, p2 ribbing.

Change to larger dpn and knit 1 rnd, purling last st. **Note:** Always purl the last st for center of underarm.

Place charted pattern so that the st marked with X is at center sleeve.

On every 6th rnd, increase 1 st on each side of centered purl st on underarm until st count is 58 (60, 60, 64, 64) and sleeve measures 22½ (23¼, 23¼, 23¾, 23¾) in / 57 (59, 59, 60, 60) cm above cast-on row.
Shape underarm as on body.

Set sleeve aside while you knit the second sleeve the same way.

RAGLAN SHAPING

The rnd now begins at center front. Arrange body and sleeves on larger circular. You will now knit the sleeves with the body, working decreases for raglan shaping, *at the same time* decreasing to shape V-neck at center front.

Note: Please read entirely through this page before you begin knitting.

Continuing in pattern:

Knit to last st before armhole on front, pm, and knit last st of front.

Knit first st on sleeve and pm.

Knit to last sleeve st, pm, knit last sleeve st and first st of back; pm.

Knit to last st of back, pm, knit last st on back, knit first st on sleeve, pm.

Knit to last sleeve st, pm, knit first st on front, pm, knit to end of front.

Knit 2 rnds without decreasing.

Note: Always decrease with main color, and always work sts between markers with contrast color.

Shape raglan by decreasing on each side of each marker as follows:

Knit until 2 sts before marker, k2tog, sl m; knit the 2 sts inside markers; sl m, sl 1, k1, psso (or ssk) = 8 decreases per rnd.

Decrease the same way on every other rnd. *At the same time*, shape V-neck.

V-NECK

Decrease at each side of steek on every 8th rnd.

On right side of steek, k2tog.

On left side of steek, sl 1, k1, psso (or ssk).

Continue shaping raglan and V-neck until piece measures 25¼ (26, 26¾, 27½, 28¼) in / 64 (66, 68, 70, 72) cm. On the last rnd, halve the st count by working k2tog around. Leave sts on circular or place on a holder. These will become part of the shawl collar.

SHAWL COLLAR AND BUTTONHOLES

With smaller circular (as for ribbing on lower edges of body and sleeves) and Ochre, pick up and knit 3 sts for every 4 sts/rows along edge for buttonhole band, so that the band won't pucker. Knit across back neck sts on holder, increasing with a few sts where you had previously decreased. Pm on the row you began shaping V-neck and on first row of raglan decreases. You will need these markers when making short rows so that the shawl collar will be longer at back neck than the button bands.

Short Rows: Begin at lower edge of button band. You should now have 4 markers along collar. The band/collar is worked in k2, p2 ribbing.

Work to the last marker from where you began the row, turn and work back. Work back to corresponding marker on opposite side.

When you now turn and work back, work to marker before the first marker you knitted at beginning of row. Turn and work back to corresponding marker on opposite side; turn and work to end of row.

Repeat this method of working on every row until you've worked 8 rows on the front bands outside the markers, so that shawl collar will be longer at back neck.

Buttonholes: *At the same time* as working the button bands and back of shawl collar, make buttonholes evenly spaced about 1½ in / 4 cm apart on left front band, from the lower edge of band and up to base of V-neck. BO 2 sts for each buttonhole, and, on the following row, CO sts over gap.

Continue working as est until you have 8 rows on
each front band and 24 rows at center of back
neck. BO on RS.

FINISHING

Reinforce steek by crocheting two lines or by
machine-stitching 2 zigzag lines on each side
of center steek st. Carefully cut open steek up
center st.
Fold steek sts to WS and either hand sew on ribbon
to cover cut edges or pick up and knit stitches
along band and knit a stockinette facing. Fold
facing over steek and cut edges on WS and sew
down. Sew 8 buttons to right button band.
Seam underarms. Weave in all ends neatly on WS.

Gently steam press cardigan under damp pressing
cloth or pat out cardigan to finished measurements on a damp towel. Cover with another
damp towel and leave until completely dry.

Chart

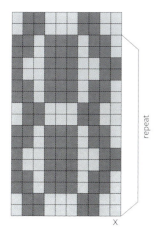

☐ Steel Gray
■ Charcoal Gray

Geysir

WOMEN'S CARDIGAN

This was one of the most used motifs for "Icelander" sweaters produced at Salhus Tricotagefabrik. The pattern frequently appeared from 1945 until 1969, often in black with red pattern colors, as seen below. The brand name was obviously inspired by Iceland and, in the 1950s, the Geysir sweaters were sold alongside their namesakes "Hekla" and "Snorre." Some years later, the pattern was also made with three colors.

Now Geyser has taken a step away from the original unisex styling and become a feminine jacket, with raglan shaping and a long ribbed lower edge to make it narrower.

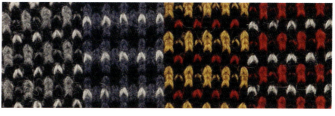

Knitted samples from 1959, 1952, and 1958.

DESIGN
Berit Løkken, Hillesvåg Ukvare fabrik

SKILL LEVEL
Experienced

SIZES
S (M, L, XL, XXL)

FINISHED MEASUREMENTS
Chest: 36¾ (39½, 42½, 45¾, 49¾) in /
93 (100, 108, 116, 126) cm
Total Length: measured down center back, 22½
(23¼, 24, 24¾, 25½) in / 57 (59, 61, 63, 65) cm
Sleeve Length: 18¼ (18½, 19, 19, 19¼) in /
46 (47, 48, 48, 49) cm

MATERIALS
Yarn:
CYCA #2 (sport, baby) Hillesvåg Ask (100%
Norwegian wool, 344 yd/315 m / 100 g)

Yarn Colors and Amounts:
MC: Dark Burgundy 316072: 350 (400, 450, 500, 550) g
CC1: Dark Terracotta Heather 316503: 50 (100, 100, 100,
150) g
CC2: Cognac 316095: 50 (50, 50, 50, 50) g

Notions:
9 (9, 9, 10, 10) buttons

Needles:
U. S. size 1.5 / 2.5 mm: circulars 16 and
32 in / 40 and 80 cm; set of 5 dpn
U. S. size 2.5 / 3 mm: circular 32 in / 80 cm; set of 5 dpn

GAUGE
24 sts x 32 rnds in stockinette pattern
on larger needles = 4 in / 10 cm.
Adjust needle size to obtain correct gauge if necessary.

BODY

With MC and smaller circular, CO 238 (256, 274,
292, 316) sts.
Work back and forth.
The outermost 10 sts at each side are the front
bands and are worked as k2, p2 (on RS, make
sure to knit the 2 outermost sts at each side).
Work the rest of the sts in pattern following Chart 1.
Begin as indicated on the chart and repeat across
(ending with p2 for front band).
When piece is 1 in / 2.5 cm long, make buttonhole, 4
sts in from edge.

Buttonholes:
BO 2 sts. CO 2 sts over the gap on next row.
Note: Space buttonholes approx. every 2½ in / 6 cm.

Continue in ribbing and pattern until piece measures
8 (8¼, 8¾, 9, 9½) in / 20 (21, 22, 23, 24) cm.
Place the outermost 10 sts at each side on a holder.
Change to larger circular.
CO 5 sts at center front for steek. Steek sts are not
worked in pattern but will later be cut open.
Work steek sts: p1, k3, p1.
Increase 1 st (all sizes) = 219 (237, 255, 273, 297)
sts + 5 steek sts.
Continue around in pattern following Chart 2 until
piece measures 13¾ (14¼, 14¼, 14½, 15) in / 35
(36, 36, 37, 38) cm.
Pm on each side with 55 (59, 63, 68, 74) sts for each
front + steek and 109 (119, 129, 137, 149) sts
for back.
BO 5 sts on each side of each marker (= 10 sts
centered on each underarm).
Set aside body while you knit sleeves.

SLEEVES

With MC and smaller dpn, CO 54 (60, 66, 66, 66) sts. Divide sts onto dpn and join.

Work around following Chart 1.

Continue in ribbing until piece is approx. 2½ (2½, 2¾, 2¾, 2¾) in / 6 (6, 7, 7, 7) cm long.

Change to larger dpn and continue in stockinette with MC

On the 1st rnd, increase 8 sts evenly spaced around.

On every 7th rnd, increase 2 sts centered on underarm until there are 94 (96, 98, 100, 102) sts. When sleeve is 18¼ (18½, 19, 19, 19¼) in / 46 (47, 48, 48, 49) cm long, BO 10 sts centered on underarm.

Set sleeve aside while you knit second sleeve the same way.

YOKE

Arrange all the pieces on larger circular, working in Chart 2 pattern on all pieces: first front, first sleeve, back, second sleeve, second front = 367 (389, 411, 433, 461) sts + steek.

Pm at each intersection of body and sleeve: between right front and sleeve; between sleeve and back; between back and second sleeve; between sleeve and left front.

RAGLAN SHAPING

Knit until 2 sts before marker 1, k2tog, sl m, k2tog tbl (or ssk); *knit until 2 sts before next marker, k2tog (= before marker), sl m, k2tog tbl (or ssk) (= after marker)*; rep from * to * around, ending with stockinette pattern to steek, work steek.

Note: Work raglan decreases with MC, but, if the entire rnd is in CC, also work decreases with CC.

Decrease the same way on every rnd a total of 3 (3, 4, 5, 6) times = 343 (365, 379, 393, 413) + steek sts rem.

Next, decrease on every other rnd 30 (31, 33, 35, 37) times = 103 (117, 115, 113, 117) + steek sts rem.

All sizes: Continue in stockinette with MC and raise back neck with short rows as follows:

Pm at center of back.

K8 sts past center marker; turn. Sl 1, p16; turn. Sl 1, k24; turn.

Sl 1, p32.

Continue turning as est, with 8 more sts before the turn until you work over 97 (113, 113, 113, 113) sts.

Turn and knit 1 rnd, decreasing evenly spaced to 98 (102, 102, 106, 106) sts.

BO the 5 steek sts. Leave rem sts on needle.

FINISHING

Reinforce steek by machine-stitching 2 zigzag lines on each side of center steek st. Carefully cut steek open up center st.

Front Bands:

Slip the 10 sts of button band from holder to smaller needles and CO 6 new sts at body side for facing. Continue in k2, p2 ribbing, but, work facing in stockinette until band is, when slightly stretched, same length as front edge. BO the 6 facing sts. Make the buttonhole band the same way, spacing buttonholes as before. The last buttonhole should be placed at neckline.

Neckband:

Slip front band and neck sts to smaller circular and continue in k2, p2 ribbing for 2¾ in / 7 cm.

BO all sts. Sew front bands to body and sew down facings on WS to cover cut edges.
Fold neckband in half to WS and sew down smoothly.
Sew on buttons and seam underarms.
Weave in all ends neatly on WS.
Pat out cardigan to finished measurements and lay on a damp towel. Cover with another damp towel and leave until completely dry. Or, lightly soak cardigan, spin out excess water in a spin dryer (centrifuge) and lay flat to dry.

Chart 1

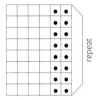

repeat

Chart 2

repeat

- ⊡ MC, purl on RS, knit on WS
- ☐ MC, knit on RS, purl on WS
- 🟨 CC2
- 🟧 CC1

Strike

UNISEX PULLOVER

Knit a dashing sweater! This is a simple "Icelander" pattern from the 1970s and '80s with simple squares and lice. It was produced in many combinations of two or three colors—take your inspiration from these samples, or choose your own colors. We knitted our version in the original colors: gray, black, and red, for a classic "Icelander" for both women and men. The pattern's easy and quick to knit, and with raglan shaping, there's little finishing work. The version shown here was knitted with Sisu but could also be made with Mini Alpakka—the gauge and colors are the same for both yarns.

Knitted samples from the 1980s.

DESIGN
Siv Dyvik

SKILL LEVEL
Experienced

SIZES
XS (S, M, L, XL, XXL)

FINISHED MEASUREMENTS
Chest: 33 (36¾, 40¼, 43¾, 47¼, 50¾) in /
84 (93, 102, 111, 120, 129) cm
Total Length: approx. 26 (26¾, 27½, 28¼, 29¼, 30) in /
66 (68, 70, 72, 74, 76) cm
Sleeve Length: approx. 19¼ (19¾, 20, 20½, 21, 21¼) in /
49 (50, 51, 52, 53, 54) cm

MATERIALS
Yarn:
CYCA #1 (fingering) Sandnes Garn Mini Alpakka
(100% alpaca, 164 yd/150 m / 50 g)
CYCA #1 (fingering) Sandnes Garn Sisu (80% wool,
20% nylon, superwash, 191 yd/175 m / 50 g)

Yarn Colors and Amounts:
Color 1: Light Gray Heather 1032: 300 (350, 350, 400,
400, 450) g
Color 2: Black 1099: 100 (100, 100, 100, 150, 150) g
Color 3: Red 4219: 50 (50, 50, 50, 100, 100) g

Needles:
U. S. sizes 1.5 and 2.5 / 2.5 and 3 mm: circulars 16 and
32 or 40 in / 40 and 80 or 100 cm; sets of 5 dpn

GAUGE
27 sts in stockinette pattern on larger
needles = 4 in / 10 cm.
Adjust needle size to obtain correct gauge if necessary.

FRONT AND BACK

With Color 1 and smaller circular, CO 228 (252, 276,
300, 324, 348) sts. Join, being careful not to
twist cast-on row; pm for beginning of rnd. Work
around in k2, p2 ribbing: 8 rnds with Color 1, 4
rnds with Color 2, and 2 rnds with Color 3.
Change to Color 1 and continue ribbing in the rnd
until piece measures 3¼ in / 8 cm.
Change to larger circular and knit 1 rnd.
Continue in the rnd and stockinette following chart
until piece measures approx. 18¼ (18½, 19, 19¼,
19¾, 20) in / 46 (47, 48, 49, 50, 51) cm, ending
after 1 rnd with Color 1 in pattern.

Divide for body and sleeves as follows:
BO the first 8 (8, 9, 9, 10, 10) sts;
k99 (111, 121, 133, 143, 155) = front;
BO next 15 (15, 17, 17, 19, 19) sts = right
underarm;
k99 (111, 121, 133, 143, 155) = back;
BO last 7 (7, 8, 8, 9, 9) sts = left underarm.
Set body aside while you knit the sleeves.

SLEEVES

With Color 1 and smaller dpn, CO 56 (56, 60, 60, 64,
64) sts. Divide sts onto dpn and join.
Work around in k2, p2 ribbing: 8 rnds with Color 1, 4
rnds with Color 2, and 2 rnds with Color 3.
Change to Color 1 and continue ribbing in the rnd
until piece measures 3¼ in / 8 cm.
Change to larger dpn and knit 1 rnd.
Continue around in stockinette following chart.
Count out from arrow indicating center of sleeve
to determine beginning st for your size. Make
sure pattern is centered on sleeve.
Note: Always purl the st at center of underarm.
Approx. every ¾ (⅝, ⅝, ⅝,⅜-⅝, ⅜-⅝) in / 2 (1.5,
1.5, 1.5, 1-1.5, 1-1,5) cm, increase 1 st on each
side of centered purl st 20 (22, 22, 24, 24, 26)
times = 96 (100, 104, 108, 112, 116) sts. *Always
work increases with Color 1.* Work new sts into
pattern as well as possible.

Continue in pattern until sleeve measures 19¼ (19¾, 20, 20½, 21, 21¼) in / 49 (50, 51, 52, 53, 54) cm or desired length.

End on same pattern row as on body.

BO the center underarm purl st + 7 (7, 8, 8, 9, 9) sts on each side of center st = 15 (15, 17, 17, 19, 19) sts bound off on underarm and 81 (85, 87, 91, 93, 97) sts rem.

Set sleeve aside while you knit second sleeve the same way.

RAGLAN SHAPING

Arrange all the pieces on larger circular: back, first sleeve, front, second sleeve = a total of 360 (392, 416, 448, 472, 504) sts.

Pm at each intersection of body and sleeve = 4 markers. Rnd now begins at back/sleeve join.

Continue in the rnd following chart. On next rnd, begin raglan shaping as follows:

K2tog after each marker and k2tog tbl (or ssk) before each marker = 8 sts decreased per rnd.

Note: The pattern will not align at decrease lines.

Repeat the decreases on every 4th rnd 3 (3, 2, 2, 1, 1) more times = 328 (360, 392, 424, 456, 488) sts rem.

Now decrease on every other rnd 20 (22, 24, 27, 30, 33) times = 168 (184, 200, 208, 216, 224) sts rem.

On next rnd, BO the center front 27 (29, 31, 33, 35, 37) sts for front neck.

Knit to beginning of rnd and cut yarn.

Beginning at center front, continue in stockinette following chart, working back and forth. At neck edge, BO 3 sts at beginning of each row and, *at the same time*, shape raglan on RS 5 (5, 6, 6, 8, 8) times more = a total of 29 (31, 33, 36, 40, 43) raglan decreases on back.

Leave rem sts on needle.

NECKBAND

With smaller circular and Color 1, pick up and knit approx. 14 sts per 2 in / 5 cm around neck. Adjust st count to approx. 136 (140, 144, 144, 148, 152) sts. The st count should be a multiple of 4.

Work around in k2, p2 ribbing: 8 rnds with Color 1, 4 rnds with Color 2, and 2 rnds with Color 3.

Change to Color 1 and continue ribbing in the rnd until piece measures 3¼ in / 8 cm.

BO loosely in ribbing.

Fold neckband in half and sew down by hand on WS.

Seam underarms.

Weave in all ends neatly on WS.

Chart

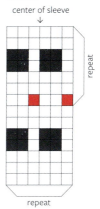

center of sleeve ↓

repeat

repeat

☐ Color 1
■ Color 2
■ Color 3

Strike

COVERLET AND PILLOW COVERS

Here's a simple and easy-to-knit "Icelander" pattern from the 1970s and '80s. The motif is used for elegant interior knitting in ochre, petroleum, and beige. On the single-color pillow cover and coverlet, the same motif is worked with knit and purl stitches for a fine and simple structure.

Don't be alarmed when you see the yarn amounts for the coverlet. The yarn is held double and you knit with large needles, so the project moves along quickly.

Pillow Cover 1.

Pillow Cover 2, Color Suggestion 1.

Pillow Cover 2, Color Suggestions 2 and 3.

DESIGN
Siv Dyvik

SKILL LEVEL
Experienced

FINISHED MEASUREMENTS
Coverlet: 43¼ x 59 in / 110 x 150 cm
Pillow Cover 1: 19¾ x 19¾ in / 50 x 50 cm
Pillow Cover 2: 17¾ x 17¾ in / 45 x 45 cm

MATERIALS
Yarn:
CYCA #2 (sport, baby) Rauma Finull PT2 (100% Norwegian wool, 191 yd/175 m / 50 g)

Yarn Colors and Amounts:
Coverlet:
Gray Beige 452: 1000 g

Pillow Cover 1:
Light Olive Green 417: 200 g

Pillow Cover 2:
Suggestion 1:
Color 1: Light Petroleum 483: 150 g
Color 2: Light Olive Green 417: 50 g
Color 3: Gray Beige 452: 50 g

Suggestion 2:
Color 1: Gray Beige 452: 150 g
Color 2: Light Petroleum 483: 50 g
Color 3: Dark Blue-Gray 4387: 50 g

Suggestion 3:
Color 1: Gray Beige 452: 150 g
Color 2: Light Olive Green 417: 50 g
Color 3: Dark Blue-Gray 4387: 50 g

Notions:
Pillow inserts:
Pillow Cover 1: 19¾ x 19¾ in / 50 x 50 cm
Pillow Cover 2: 17¾ x 17¾ in / 45 x 45 cm

Needles:

Coverlet: U. S. size 8 / 5 mm: circular
32 or 40 in / 80 or 100 cm
Pillow Covers 1 and 2: U. S. size 2.5
/ 3 mm: circular 24 in / 60 cm

GAUGE

Coverlet: 16 sts in ribbed pattern = 4 in / 10 cm.
Pillow Cover 1: 22 sts in ribbed pattern = 4 in / 10 cm.
Pillow Cover 2: 24 sts in stockinette pattern = 4 in / 10 cm.
Adjust needle size to obtain correct gauge if necessary.

COVERLET

With *two strands of yarn held together*, CO 176 sts.
Work back and forth following Chart 1 until piece is
approx. 59 in / 150 cm long.
End with a complete pattern repeat.
BO loosely on last row.

FRINGE

Each fringe: 5 strands that will be about 4 in / 10 cm
long when knotted. See page 267 for details.
Knot fringe along the cast-on and bind-off rows.

PILLOW COVER 1

CO 210 sts. Join, being careful not to twist cast-on
row; pm for beginning of rnd.
Knit around following Chart 2 until piece is about
19¼ in / 49 cm long.
End with a complete pattern repeat.
BO loosely on next rnd.

Seam cover on one end.
Insert pillow form and seam other end.

PILLOW COVER 2

With Color 1, CO 210 sts. Join, being careful not to
twist cast-on row; pm for beginning of rnd.

Knit around following Chart 3 until piece is about
17¼ in / 44 cm long.
End with a complete pattern repeat.
BO loosely on next rnd.

Seam cover on one end.
Insert pillow form and seam other end.

Chart 1

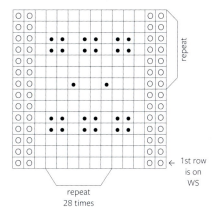

repeat

← 1st row
is on
WS

repeat
28 times

Chart 2

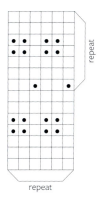

repeat

repeat

Chart 3

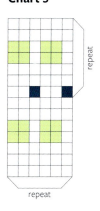

repeat

repeat

Charts 1 + 2

☐ Knit on RS, purl on WS
• Purl on RS, knit on WS
⊙ Edge st, always knit on all rows

Chart 3

☐ Color 1
☐ Color 2
■ Color 3

The Worker

UNISEX PULLOVER

An "Icelander" from Salhus Tricotagefabrik in green, charcoal, and natural white.

This sweater is a relative of the traditional "Icelander" patterns, with two lice separated by a square. Most of our knitted samples of this motif are undated, but we believe it was used in the 1980s. The pullover is in homage to working people of all types, and to the "Icelander" as a working garment through time, whether brand new or well-felted and mended here and there.

Originally, this sweater was often knitted with an overall pattern in white, red, and black, with striped ribbing (Color Suggestion 2). We've also included an alternate version with a single-color section at the top and single-color ribbing (Color Suggestion 1).

Knitted samples from the 1980s.

DESIGN
Berit Løkken, Hillesvåg Ullvarefabrikk

SKILL LEVEL
Experienced

SIZES
S (M, L, XL, XXL)

FINISHED MEASUREMENTS
Chest: 38½ (41¼, 45¾, 49¼, 52¾) in
/ 98 (105, 116, 125, 134) cm
Total Length: approx. 26 (26½, 27½, 28¾, 29¼) in /
66 (67, 70, 73, 74) cm
Sleeve Length: 19¼ (19¼, 19¾, 20, 20) in /
49 (49, 50, 51, 51) cm

MATERIALS
Yarn:

CYCA #2 (sport, baby) Hillesvåg Sol Lamullgarn (100%
Norwegian lamb's wool, 317 yd/290 m / 100 g)
CYCA #3 (DK, light worsted) Hillesvåg Tinde Pelsullgarn
(100% Norwegian wool, 284 yd/260 m / 100 g)

Yarn Colors and Amounts:
Suggestion 1:
MC: Sol, Natural White 58400: 250 (300, 350, 350, 400) g
CC1: Tinde, Petroleum 652105: 200 (200, 250, 250, 300) g
CC2: Tinde, Natural Gray 652115: 100 (150, 150, 150,
200) g

Suggestion 2:
MC: Sol, Natural White 58400: 300 (300, 350, 400, 450) g
CC1: Tinde, Black 652109: 150 (150, 200, 200, 250) g
CC2: Sol, Red 58406: 150 (150, 150, 200, 200) g

Needles:
U. S. size 2.5 / 3 mm: set of 5 dpn
U. S. size 6 / 4 mm: circulars 16 and 32
in / 40 and 80 cm; set of 5 dpn
If you knit stranded colorwork tightly, use
U. S. size 7 / 4.5 mm for those sections

GAUGE
22 sts x 29 rnds in stockinette pattern
on larger needles = 4 in / 10 cm.
Adjust needle size to obtain correct gauge if necessary.

BODY
Color Suggestion 1:
With CC1 and smaller circular, CO 212 (228, 252,
272, 292) sts.
Join, being careful not to twist cast-on row; pm for
beginning of rnd.
Work around in k2, p2 ribbing for approx. 2½ in / 6
cm (all sizes).
On the last rnd of ribbing, increase 3 (2, 3, 3, 3) sts
evenly spaced around to 215 (230, 255, 275,
295) sts.
Change to larger circular and continue in stockinette
and stripes as follows:
2 rnds with CC1, 2 rnds with CC2, 2 rnds with CC1.

Color Suggestion 2:
With CC1 and smaller circular, CO 212 (228, 252,
272, 292) sts.
Join, being careful not to twist cast-on row; pm for
beginning of rnd.
Work around in k2, p2 ribbing in stripes as follows:
5 rnds with CC1, 5 rnds with CC2, 8 rnds with CC1.
On the last rnd of ribbing, increase 3 (2, 3, 3, 3) sts
evenly spaced around to 215 (230, 255, 275,
295) sts.
Change to larger circular.

Both Color Suggestions:
Continue in pattern following chart (if you knit
colorwork tightly, change to U. S. 7 / 4.5 mm
circular).
Begin as shown on chart and then work repeat.
When body measures 17¼ (17¼, 17¾, 18¼, 18¼)
in / 44 (44, 45, 46, 46) cm, pm on each side of
body, with 107 (115, 127, 137, 147) sts for front
and 108 (115, 128, 138, 148) sts for back.
End with a complete repeat, on the same row for
body and sleeves.
BO 6 sts on each side of each side marker (= 12 sts
bound off for each underarm).
Set body aside while you knit sleeves.

SLEEVES

With CC1 and smaller dpn, CO 48 (52, 52, 56, 60) sts. Divide sts onto dpn and join. Work around in k2, p2 ribbing as for lower edge of body.

On the last rnd of ribbing, increase evenly spaced around to 55 (55, 55, 60, 65) sts.

Change to larger dpn.

Suggestion 1:

Continue in stockinette and stripes as follows:
2 rnds with CC1, 2 rnds with CC2, 2 rnds with CC1.

Both Color Suggestions:

Continue in pattern following chart (if you knit colorwork tightly, change to U. S. 7 / 4.5 mm dpn).

Begin as shown on chart and then continue with repeat.

On every 5th rnd, increase 2 sts centered on underarm until there are 95 (97, 101, 104, 107) sts. When sleeve is 19¼ (19¼, 19¾, 20, 20) in / 49 (49, 50, 51, 51) cm long, BO 12 sts centered on underarm.

End with a complete repeat, on the same row for body.

Set sleeve aside while you knit second sleeve the same way.

RAGLAN SHAPING

Arrange all the pieces on larger circular as follows: back, first sleeve, front, second sleeve = 357 (376, 409, 435, 461) sts.

Continue in pattern and, at the same time, shape raglan:

Pm at each intersection of body and sleeve. The rnd now begins at beginning of back.

Note: Work all raglan decreases with MC.

Knit until 2 sts before marker, *k2tog tbl (or ssk), sl m, k2tog; knit until 2 sts before next marker*; rep * to * around.

Decrease the same way on every rnd a total of 3 (4, 4, 5, 5) times = 333 (344, 377, 395, 421) sts rem.

Color Suggestion 1:

Decrease on every other rnd until 197 (208, 217, 219, 221) sts rem = 17 (17, 20, 22, 25) times.

At the same time, work stripes as you continue raglan shaping: 2 rnds with CC1, 2 rnds with CC2, and then continue with CC1.

Continue raglan shaping until 141 (144, 145, 147, 149) sts rem = 7 (8, 9, 9, 9) times since last count of rem sts and decrease times count.

Color Suggestion 2:

Decrease on every other rnd 141 (144, 145, 147, 149) sts rem = 24 (25, 29, 31, 34) times.

Both Versions:

BO center 27 (29, 31, 33, 33) sts of front (or place sts on a holder) and work back and forth in stockinette (single color or pattern).

At the same time, at neck edge on every other row, BO 3, 2, 1, 1, 1 sts (or place sts on a holder).

Continue raglan shaping as est.

Now work neckband.

NECKBAND

With CC1 and smaller circular, pick up and knit sts around neck, including those on holder.

Work 1 rnd in stockinette, adjusting stitch count to 108 (112, 112, 116, 116) sts total, spacing increases/decreases evenly around.

Color Suggestion 1:

Work around in k2, p2 ribbing for approx. 2¾ in / 7 cm.

Color Suggestion 2:

Work around in k2, p2 ribbing and stripes as follows: 3 rnds CC1, 3 rnds CC2; continue with CC1 until neckband measures approx. 2¾ in / 7 cm.

FINISHING
Both Versions:

BO rem sts in ribbing.

Fold neckband in half and sew down edge on WS.

Seam underarms.

Weave in all ends neatly on WS.

Pat out sweater to finished measurements on a damp towel. Cover with another damp towel and leave until completely dry.

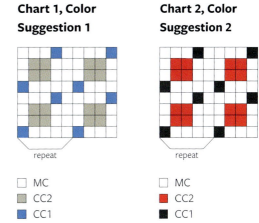

Chart 1, Color Suggestion 1

repeat

☐ MC
⬜ CC2
🟦 CC1

Chart 2, Color Suggestion 2

repeat

☐ MC
🟥 CC2
⬛ CC1

Makko

UNISEX PULLOVER

Makko, or máko, is Egyptian cotton, which was much used for knitting undergarments and stockings in the golden age of the Norwegian textile industry. It was the raw material for the best-known brand at Salhus Tricotagefabrik: Krone-Maco cotton undergarments. For a while, the term was used so much that it became a general word for long cotton underpants, in Norwegian.

The pullover shown here was knitted with soft alpaca rather than Egyptian cotton. It suits everyone and can be made with either a high or low neckband. The pattern forms a striking look in black and white, and dates to between 1910 and 1920. If you would rather have a wool sweater, you can knit it with Sisu—the gauge and colors are the same as for the alpaca yarn.

Label for
Krone Maco
undergarments.

Knitted samples from between 1910 and 1920.

DESIGN
Siv Dyvik

SKILL LEVEL
Experienced

SIZES
XS (S, M, L, XL, XXL)

FINISHED MEASUREMENTS
Chest: 33 (36¾, 40¼, 43¾, 47¼, 50¾) in
/ 84 (93, 102, 111, 120, 129) cm
Total Length: approx. 26 (26¾, 27½, 28¼, 29¼, 30) in /
66 (68, 70, 72, 74, 76) cm
Sleeve Length: approx. 19¼ (19¾, 20, 20½, 21, 21¼) in /
49 (50, 51, 52, 53, 54) cm or desired length

MATERIALS
Yarn:

CYCA #1 (fingering) Sandnes Garn Mini Alpakka
(100% alpaca, 164 yd/150 m / 50 g)
CYCA #1 (fingering) Sandnes Garn Sisu (80% wool,
20% nylon, superwash, 191 yd/175 m / 50 g)

Yarn Colors and Amounts:
Suggestion 1:
Color 1: Black 1099: 300 (350, 350, 400, 400, 450) g
Color 2: White 1001: 150 (150, 200, 200, 250, 250) g
+ 50 g extra of Color 1 for high neck.

Suggestion 2:
Color 1: White 1001: 300 (350, 350, 400, 400, 450) g
Color 2: Black 1099: 150 (150, 200, 200, 250, 250) g
+ 50 g extra of Color 1 for high neck.

Needles:
U. S. sizes 1.5 and 2.5 / 2.5 and 3 mm: circulars
32 or 40 in / 80 or 100 cm; set of 5 dpn
+ 16 or 24 in / 40 or 60 cm smaller circular for neckband

GAUGE
27 sts in stockinette or pattern on
larger needles = 4 in / 10 cm.
Adjust needle size to obtain correct gauge if necessary.

FRONT AND BACK

With Color 1 and smaller circular, CO 228 (252, 276,
300, 324, 348) sts. Join, being careful not to
twist cast-on row; pm for beginning of rnd. Work
around in k2, 2 ribbing for 2½ in / 6 cm.
Change to larger circular and knit 1 rnd.
Now work around in stockinette pattern following
chart until piece measures approx.18¼ (18¾, 19,
19¼, 19¾, 20) in / 46 (47, 48, 49, 50, 51) cm.
ending after a rnd with Color 1 in pattern.
Divide for body and sleeves as follows:
BO 8 (8, 9, 9, 10, 10) sts; k99 (111, 121, 133,
143, 155) = front, BO next 15 (15, 17, 17, 19,
19) sts = right underarm; k99 (111, 121, 133,
143, 155) = back; BO rem 7 (7, 8, 8, 9, 9) sts.
Set body aside while you knit sleeves.

SLEEVES

With Color 1 and smaller dpn, CO 56 (56, 60, 60, 64,
64) sts. Divide sts onto dpn and join.
Work around in k2, 2 ribbing for 2½ in / 6 cm.
Change to larger dpn and knit 1 rnd.
Continue around in stockinette pattern following
chart. Count out from arrow on chart for center
of sleeve to determine starting point for your
size. Make sure pattern is centered on sleeve.
Note: Always purl st at center of underarm with
Color 1.
Increase 1 st on each side of centered purl st approx.
every ¾ (⅝, ⅝, ⅝, ⅜-⅝, ⅜-⅝) in / 2 (1.5, 1.5,
1.5, 1-1.5, 1-1.5) cm 20 (22, 22, 24, 24, 26)
times = 96 (100, 104, 108, 112, 116) sts. Work
new sts into pattern as well as possible.
Continue until sleeve is 19¼ (19¾, 20, 20½, 21,
21¼) in / 49 (50, 51, 52, 53, 54) cm long or
desired length. End on the same pattern row as
for body.
Shape underarms: BO the center st + 7 (7, 8, 8, 9,
9) sts on each side of center underarm st = 15
(15, 17, 17, 19, 19) sts bound off for underarm
and 81 (85, 87, 91, 93, 97) sts rem.

Set sleeve aside while you knit the second sleeve the same way.

RAGLAN SHAPING

Arrange all the pieces on larger circular as follows and, *at the same time*, k2tog at each intersection of body and sleeve (joining a last and first tog) = 4 sts decreased.

Back, first sleeve, front, second sleeve = 356 (388, 412, 444, 468, 500) sts total. Pm around 5 sts at each intersection of body and sleeve = marked sts. The rnd now begins at a join on the back.

Continue around with Color 1 and knit 1 rnd *but* work the marked sts on this and all subsequent rnds as: p1, k3, p1. Begin raglan decreases on next rnd:

K2tog after marked sts and k2tog tbl (or ssk) before marked sts = 8 sts decreased per rnd.

Decrease the same way on every 4th rnd 3 (3, 2, 2, 1, 1) times more = 324 (356, 388, 420, 452, 484) sts rem.

Now decrease on every other rnd 20 (22, 24, 27, 30, 33) times = 164 (180, 196, 204, 212, 220) sts rem.

On the next rnd, BO the center front 27 (29, 31, 33, 35, 37) sts for neck.

Knit to beginning of rnd and cut yarn.

Beginning at center front, continue in stockinette, working back and forth and, at neck edge, BO 3 sts at beginning of every row. *At the same time*, continue shaping raglan on RS rows 5 (5, 6, 6, 8, 8) times more = a total of 29 (31, 33, 36, 40, 43) raglan decrease rows.

Leave rem sts on circular.

NECKBAND

Short Neck:

With Color 1 and smaller circular, pick up and knit about 14 sts per 2 in / 5 cm around rest of neck

Adjust stitch count to approx. 136 (140, 144, 144, 148, 152) sts. The stitch count must be a multiple of 4 sts.

Work around in k2, p2 ribbing for approx. 1½ in / 3.5 cm. BO loosely in ribbing.

High Neck:

Work as for short neck but continue ribbing until it is approx. 8¾ in / 22 cm long.

BO loosely in ribbing.

Fold neckband forward (see photos).

FINISHING

Seam underarms.

Weave in all ends neatly on WS.

Chart

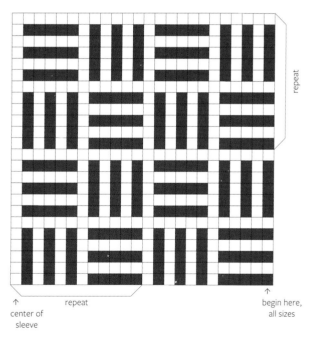

↑
center of
sleeve

repeat

↑
begin here,
all sizes

repeat

Color Suggestion 1
☐ Color 1: Black
■ Color 2: White

Color Suggestion 2
☐ Color 1: White
■ Color 2: Black

Bertel MEN'S PULLOVER

There's a lot to be said for keeping it simple. This stripe pattern is totally straightforward, but the dark stripe underneath adds a nice shadow effect. The original pattern was used in the second half of the 1920s, in colors typical of the time: beige heather, blue or yellow, and dark brown. We've kept the original colors and added a simple construction with raglan shaping and your choice of with either a round or V-neck (as shown here).

Our sweater is named for Bertel Steffensen (1844-1924) who worked at the Salhus Tricotagefabrik at the end of the nineteenth century. Together with his wife, Marta, he lived in the first workers' residence built by the factory, which stood ready for occupancy in 1860.[14]

Knitted samples from the 1920s.

DESIGN
Siv Dyvik

SKILL LEVEL
Experienced

SIZES
XS (S, M, L, XL, XXL, XXXL)

FINISHED MEASUREMENTS
Chest: 35 (37¾, 41, 43¾, 47, 49¾, 52½) in /
89 (96, 104, 111, 119, 126, 133) cm
Total Length: approx. 26½ (26¾, 27¼, 27½, 28,
28¼, 28¾) in / 67 (68, 69, 70, 71, 72, 73) cm
Sleeve Length: approx. 21¼ (21¼, 21¼, 21¾, 21¾, 21¾,
21¾) in / 54 (54, 54, 55, 55, 55, 55) cm or desired length

MATERIALS
Yarn:
CYCA #1 (fingering) Sandnes Garn Mini Alpakka
(100% alpaca, 164 yd/150 m / 50 g)

Yarn Colors and Amounts:
Color 1: Gray-Beige Heather 2650: 250 (250, 300, 300,
350, 350, 400) g
Color 2: Petroleum 6554: 150 (150, 150, 150, 200, 200,
200) g
Color 3: Dark Brown 4071: 100 (100, 100, 100, 100, 150,
150) g

Needles:
U. S. sizes 1.5 and 2.5 / 2.5 and 3 mm: circulars
32 or 40 in / 80 or 100 cm; set of 5 dpn
+ 16 or 24 in / 40 or 60 cm smaller circular for neckband

GAUGE
27 sts in stockinette or pattern on
larger needles = 4 in / 10 cm.
Adjust needle size to obtain correct gauge if necessary.

FRONT AND BACK

With Color 1 and smaller circular, CO 240 (260, 280, 300, 320, 340, 360) sts. Join, being careful not to twist cast-on row; pm for beginning of rnd.

Work around in k2, p2 ribbing for 1½ in / 4 cm.

Change to larger circular and knit 1 rnd.

Now work around in stockinette pattern following chart until piece measures approx.18¼ (18¼, 18¼, 18¼, 18½, 18½, 18½) in /46 (46, 46, 46, 47, 47, 47) cm, ending with 2nd rnd with Color 1 in pattern.

On next rnd, divide for body and sleeves as follows: BO 6 (6, 6, 6, 6, 6, 6) sts; k108 (118, 128, 138, 148, 158, 168) = front, BO next 12 (12, 12, 12, 12, 12, 12) sts = right underarm; k108 (118, 128, 138, 148, 158, 168) = back; BO rem 6 (6, 6, 6, 6, 6) sts.

Set body aside while you knit sleeves.

SLEEVES

With Color 1 and smaller dpn, CO 60 (64, 64, 68, 68, 72, 72) sts. Divide sts onto dpn and join.

Work around in k2, p2 ribbing for 1½ in / 4 cm.

Change to larger dpn and knit 1 rnd.

Continue around in stockinette pattern following chart.

Every 1 in / 2.5 cm (all sizes), increase 1 st on after first st and before last st of rnd 17 (16, 18, 18, 20, 20, 21) times = 94 (96, 100, 104, 108, 112, 114) sts.

Continue until sleeve is 21¼ (21¼, 21¼, 21¾, 21¾, 21¾, 21¾) in / 54 (54, 54, 55, 55, 55, 55) cm long or desired length. End with the 2nd rnd with Color 1 as for body.

Shape underarms: BO the center 12 sts of underarm (all sizes) = 82 (84, 88, 92, 96, 100, 102) sts rem.

Set sleeve aside while you knit the second sleeve the same way.

RAGLAN SHAPING

Round Neck:

Arrange all the pieces on larger circular as follows: back, first sleeve, front, second sleeve = 380 (404, 432, 460, 488, 516, 540) sts total. Pm at each intersection of body and sleeve = 4 markers. The rnd now begins at a join on the back.

Continue stripe pattern as est; knit 1 rnd with Color 3 and decrease 0 (0, 0, 8, 16, 16, 24) sts evenly spaced on the 1st rnd = 380 (404, 432, 452, 472, 500, 516) sts.

Begin raglan decreases on next rnd:

K2tog after each marker and k2tog tbl (or ssk) before each marker = 8 sts decreased per rnd.

Decrease the same way on every other rnd a total of 25 (27, 30, 32, 34, 37, 39) times = 180 (188, 192, 196, 200, 204, 204) sts rem.

On the next rnd, BO the center front 26 (28, 30, 32, 34, 36, 36) sts for neck.

Knit to beginning of rnd and cut yarn.

Beginning at center front, continue in stockinette stripe pattern, working back and forth and, at neck edge, BO 2 sts at beginning of *every row*. *At the same time*, continue shaping raglan on RS rows as far as possible = a total of 33 (35, 38 40, 42, 45, 47) raglan decrease rows on back.

Leave rem sts on circular.

NECKBAND

Round Neck:

With Color 1 and smaller circular, pick up and knit about 14 sts per 2 in / 5 cm around rest of neck. Adjust stitch count to approx. 120 (124, 128, 132, 136, 140, 144) sts. The stitch count must be a multiple of 4 sts.

Work around in k2, p2 ribbing for approx. 3¼ in / 8 cm. BO loosely in ribbing.

Fold neckband in half and smoothly sew down edge on WS.

FINISHING

Seam underarms.

RAGLAN SHAPING

V-Neck:

Please read entirely through this section before you begin knitting.

Arrange all the pieces on larger circular as follows: back, first sleeve, front, second sleeve = 380 (404, 432, 460, 488, 516, 540) sts total.

Pm at each intersection of body and sleeve = 4 markers. The rnd now begins at a join on the back.

Continue stripe pattern as est; knit 1 rnd with Color 3 and decrease 0 (0, 0, 8, 16, 16, 24) sts evenly spaced on the 1st rnd = 380 (404, 432, 452, 472, 500, 516) sts rem.

Begin raglan decreases on next rnd:

K2tog after each marker and k2tog tbl (or ssk) before each marker = 8 sts decreased per rnd.

Decrease the same way on every other rnd, but, when piece measures approx. 2 (2, 2½, 2½, 2½, 2¾, 2¾) in / 5 (5, 6, 6, 6, 7, 7) cm from first raglan decrease rnd, BO the 2 center front sts.

Knit to beginning of rnd and cut yarn.

Now begin at center front and work stripe pattern back and forth.

Shape V-neck: Decrease 1 st at beginning of *every* row. *At the same time,* continue shaping raglan on RS rows as long as possible, and until there have been a total of 33 (35, 38 40, 42, 45, 47) raglan decrease rows on the back.

Leave rem sts on circular.

NECKBAND

V-Neck:

Beginning at center front, with Color 1 and smaller circular, pick up and knit approx. 14 sts per 2 in / 5 cm up right side of neck, knit across back neck, and pick up and knit sts down left side (make sure you have the same number of sts on right and left sides). The stitch count must be a multiple of 4.

The rnd begins at center front (base of V).

Work around as follows: K1, (p2, k2) around, ending with p2, k1.

On every other rnd, decrease 1 st after first and before last st.

Continue in ribbing with decreases as est until band measures about 1½ in / 4 cm.

BO loosely in ribbing.

FINISHING

Seam underarms.

Weave in all ends neatly on WS.

Chart

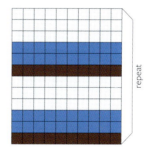

☐ Color 1: Gray-Beige Heather
🟦 Color 2: Petroleum
🟫 Color 3: Dark Brown

Astri WOMEN'S PULLOVER

Here's a variation in women's sizes of the striped pullover described on the previous pages. The women's pullover has raglan shaping, a simple round neck, and new colors of petroleum and rust. With a simple pattern and slightly larger needles, it's a project you can get really going on. The sweater name honors Astri Falkanger, a seamstress at Salhus Tricotagefabrik from 1962 until it closed down in 1989.

Astri demonstrates how she usually sewed undergarments at the factory, here at a museum event.

DESIGN
Siv Dyvik

SKILL LEVEL
Experienced

SIZES
Women's S (M, L, XL)

FINISHED MEASUREMENTS
Chest: 34¾ (37¾, 41, 44) in / 88 (96, 104, 112) cm
Total Length: approx. 22 (22¾, 23¾, 24½) in /
56 (58, 60, 62) cm
Sleeve Length: approx. 18¼ (18½, 18½, 19) in /
46 (47, 47, 48) cm or desired length

MATERIALS
Yarn:

CYCA #1 (fingering) Sandnes Garn Mini Alpakka
(100% alpaca, 164 yd/150 m / 50 g)

Yarn Colors and Amounts:

Color 1: Dusty Petroleum 7212: 200 (250, 250, 300) g
Color 2: Petroleum 6554: 150 (150, 150, 150) g
Color 3: Rust 3355: 100 (100, 100, 100) g

Needles:

U. S. sizes 2.5 and 4 / 3 and 3.5 mm: circulars
32 or 40 in / 80 or 100 cm; set of 5 dpn
+ 16 or 24 in / 40 or 60 cm smaller circular for neckband

GAUGE
25 sts in stockinette or pattern on
larger needles = 4 in / 10 cm.
Adjust needle size to obtain correct gauge if necessary.

Chart

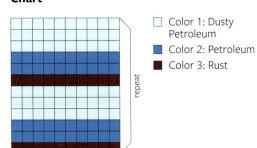

☐ Color 1: Dusty Petroleum
■ Color 2: Petroleum
■ Color 3: Rust

repeat

FRONT AND BACK

With Color 2 and smaller circular, CO 240 (260, 280, 300) sts. Join, being careful not to twist cast-on row; pm for beginning of rnd.

Work around in k2, p2 ribbing for 2 in / 5 cm.

Change to larger circular. Knit 1 rnd, and, *at the same time*, decrease 20 sts evenly spaced around = 220 (240, 260, 280) sts rem.

Continue around in stockinette stripe pattern following chart until piece measures approx. 15¾ in / 40 cm.

On next rnd, divide for body and sleeves as follows: BO 5 (6, 7, 8) sts; k100 (108, 116, 124) = front, BO next 10 (12, 14, 16) sts = right underarm; k100 (108, 116, 124) = back; BO rem 5 (6, 7, 8) sts.

Set body aside while you knit sleeves.

SLEEVES

With Color 2 and smaller dpn, CO 60 (64, 64, 68) sts. Divide sts onto dpn and join.

Work around in k2, p2 ribbing for 2 in / 5 cm.

Change to larger dpn and knit 1 rnd, *at the same time* decreasing 0 (2, 2, 0) sts evenly spaced around = 60 (62, 64, 66) sts.

Continue around in stockinette pattern following chart.

Approx. every 1¾ (1½, 1½, 1¼) in / 4.5 (4, 4, 3.5) cm, increase 1 st on after first st and before last st of rnd 8 (9, 10, 11) times = 76 (80, 84, 88) sts.

Continue until sleeve is approx. 18¼ (18½, 18½, 19) in / 46 (47, 47, 48) cm long or desired length. End with same row of chart as for front and back.

Shape underarms: BO the center 10 (12, 14, 16) sts of underarm = 66 (68, 70, 72) sts rem.

Set sleeve aside while you knit the second sleeve the same way.

RAGLAN SHAPING

Arrange all the pieces on larger circular as follows: back, first sleeve, front, second sleeve = 332 (352, 372, 392) sts total. Pm at each intersection of body and sleeve = 4 markers. The rnd now begins at a join on the back.

Continue stripe pattern as est and, *at the same time*, begin raglan shaping as follows:

K2tog after each marker and k2tog tbl (or ssk) before each marker = 8 sts decreased per rnd.

Decrease the same way on every 4th rnd a total of 10 (12, 14, 16) times = 252 (256, 260, 264) sts rem.

On the next rnd, BO the center front 22 sts (all sizes) for neck.

Knit to beginning of rnd and cut yarn.

Beginning at center front, continue in stockinette stripe pattern, working back and forth and, at neck edge, BO 2 sts at beginning of *every* row. *At the same time*, continue shaping raglan on RS rows as far as possible = a total of 22 (24, 26, 28) raglan decrease rows on back.

BO rem sts loosely.

NECKBAND

Begin at one shoulder.

With Color 2 and smaller circular, pick up and knit about 168 (172, 176, 180) sts around neck. The stitch count must be a multiple of 4 sts.

Work around in k2, p2 ribbing for approx. 1½ in / 4 cm. BO loosely in ribbing.

FINISHING

Seam underarms.

Weave in all ends neatly on WS.

Emil

MEN'S CARDIGAN

Emil is a handsome men's cardigan, named for Emil Clausen, son of factory founder Phillip Christian Clausen; he took over the business from his father in 1909 and ran it until he died in 1967.

The pattern motif was used in the 1960s and knitted in various gray tones with red or yellow dots between the blocks. It's reminiscent of Faroese fishermen's sweater patterns, but Salhus put its own twist on the design. This new design has solid green sleeves, and the motif appears only on the body. The cardigan can easily be knitted in colors closer to the original, using light and dark gray for the pattern squares and a contrasting color for the dots, sleeves, and ribbing.

Knitted samples from 1959 and 1960.

Emil Clausen inspects new pipelines and dam building in the mountain above the factory in 1923.

DESIGN

Berit Løkken, Hillesvåg Ullvarefabrikk

SKILL LEVEL

Experienced

SIZES

S (M, L, XL, XXL)

FINISHED MEASUREMENTS

Chest: 39 (42½, 45¾, 48¾, 52½) in /
99 (108, 116, 124, 133) cm
Total Length: as measured down center back, 26
(26½, 27½, 28¾, 29¼) in / 66 (67, 70, 73, 74) cm
Sleeve Length: 19 (19¼, 19¾, 20, 20) in /
48 (49, 50, 51, 51) cm

MATERIALS

Yarn:

CYCA #2 (sport, baby) Hillesvåg Ask (100%
Norwegian wool, 344 yd/315 m / 100 g)

Yarn Colors and Amounts:

MC: Olive-Green 316090 250 (300, 300, 350, 350) g
CC1: Natural White 316057: 150 (200, 200, 250, 250) g
CC2: Medium Gray 316055: 150 (200, 200, 200, 250) g

Notions:

10 (10, 10, 11, 11) buttons

Needles:

U. S. sizes 1.5 and 2.5 / 2.5 and 3 mm: circulars
16 and 32 in / 40 and 80 cm; sets of 5 dpn
If you knit stranded colorwork tightly, use
U. S. size 4 / 3.5 mm for those sections.

GAUGE

24 sts x 29 rnds in stockinette pattern
on larger needles = 4 in / 10 cm.
Adjust needle size to obtain correct gauge if necessary.

BODY

With MC and smaller circular, CO 254 (274, 294, 314, 334) sts. Work back and forth in k2, p2 ribbing for approx. 3¼ in / 8 cm* (all sizes).
*When ribbing is 1¼ in / 3 cm long, make a buttonhole (on the right side for women and left side for men).
Buttonhole: BO 2 sts, 6 sts in from edge (= work 6 sts, BO 2) and CO 2 new sts over the gap on the following row.
After completing ribbing, place 12 sts at each side on a holder for the front bands.
CO 5 new sts at center front for the steek. These sts will later be reinforced and cut open. Work steek as: p1, k3, p1 to mark the lines for later stitching and cutting.
All sizes: CO 1 st = CO 231 (251, 271, 291, 311) + steek sts.
Change to larger circular and begin working around in pattern following chart. If you knit two-color patterns tightly, go up to U. S. size 4 / 3.5 mm circular.
Begin and then work repeats as shown on chart.
Pm on each side of body when it is 2¾ in / 7 cm shorter than total body length with 57 (62, 67, 72, 77) + steek sts for each front and 117 (127, 137, 147, 157) sts for back.
BO the 5 steek sts and 13 (14, 15, 15, 15) sts on each side for front neck. Now work back and forth.
BO 3, 2, 2, 1, 1, 1 sts (all sizes) on each side at neck edge on every other row.
When piece is approx. 1¼ in / 3 cm shorter than total length, change to smaller circular and continue with 2 rows in MC and then continue in CC2 only.
When piece is approx. ¾ in / 2 cm shorter than total length, BO the center 39 (41, 43, 43, 43) sts for back neck and work each side separately.
At back neck edge, BO 3, then 2 sts (all sizes).
When piece is at total length, BO rem sts.
Work opposite side of neck to correspond.

SLEEVES

With MC and smaller dpn, CO 52 (56, 56, 60, 64) sts. Divide sts onto dpn and join. Work around in k2, p2 ribbing for 3¼ in / 8 cm (all sizes). On the last rnd, increase evenly spaced around to 57 (61, 63, 65, 67) sts.

Change to larger dpn and continue in stockinette.

On every 5th rnd, increase 1 st after first and 1 st before last st of rnd until there are 99 (101, 105, 109, 113) sts.

When sleeve is 19 (19¼, 19¾, 20, 20) in / 48 (49, 50, 51, 51) cm long, knit 2 rnds with CC2.

Turn sleeve inside out and knit around for 1 in / 2.5 cm long for facing.

BO loosely.

Set sleeve aside while you knit the second sleeve the same way.

FINISHING

Reinforce steek by machine-stitching 2 zigzag lines on each side of center steek st. Carefully cut open steek up center st.

Gently steam press sweater on WS under a damp pressing cloth.

Measure across (not around) top of sleeve and measure down that amount to mark armhole depth at each side.

Machine-stitch 2 lines on each side of center armhole st. Carefully cut open up center st.

Join shoulders. Attach sleeves.

FRONT BANDS

Slip the 12 sts of button band from holder to smaller circular and CO 6 new sts at body side for facing. With MC, continue in k2, p2 ribbing, but, work facing in stockinette until band is, when slightly stretched, same length as front edge.

BO the 6 facing sts. Place rem band sts on a holder.

Make the buttonhole band the same way, evenly spacing buttonholes. The top buttonhole will be on the neckband. The rest are spaced evenly

down the band. There are a total of 10 (10, 10, 11, 11) buttonholes.

When both bands are finished, slip rem band sts to smaller circular and pick up and knit approx. 126 (130, 130, 134, 134) sts around back neck.

Continue in k2, p2 ribbing back and forth for 1½ in 3.5 cm—don't forget the top buttonhole.

BO the outermost 12 sts at each side and then continue in k2, p2 ribbing for 1½ in / 3.5 cm.

BO rem sts in ribbing.

Sew the front bands to the body, sewing down facings on WS to cover cut edges from steek.

Fold neckband in half and smoothly sew down edge on WS.

Weave in all ends neatly on WS.

Sew on buttons.

BLOCKING

Pat out sweater to finished measurements on a damp towel. Place a damp towel on top and leave until sweater is completely dry. Or, spin the sweater in a spin-dryer (centrifuge) to remove excess water before laying it out to dry.

Chart

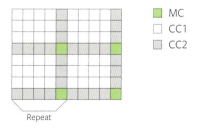

Repeat

- ■ MC
- □ CC1
- ■ CC2

Dorthea

WOMEN'S HAT AND HALF-GLOVES

Dorthea Holme (1838-1934) was born on Osterøy, Norway, and worked at the textile factory in Salhus from around 1870 until 1920.[15] We gave her name to this multi-color pattern, which was part of the "Icelander" production around the 1980s. We've featured the motif on a hat and half-gloves set. Simple "lice" lines in four pattern colors make vertical stripes in the pieces, and are repeated in the ribbing for an attractive color fade effect. Finull yarn really lets this color palette shine, but the design is also well suited to leftover yarns in varying shades of the same color. There are two color alternatives—one in blue, and the other in classic shades of gray. The multi-color pattern makes the hat and half-gloves nice and warm.

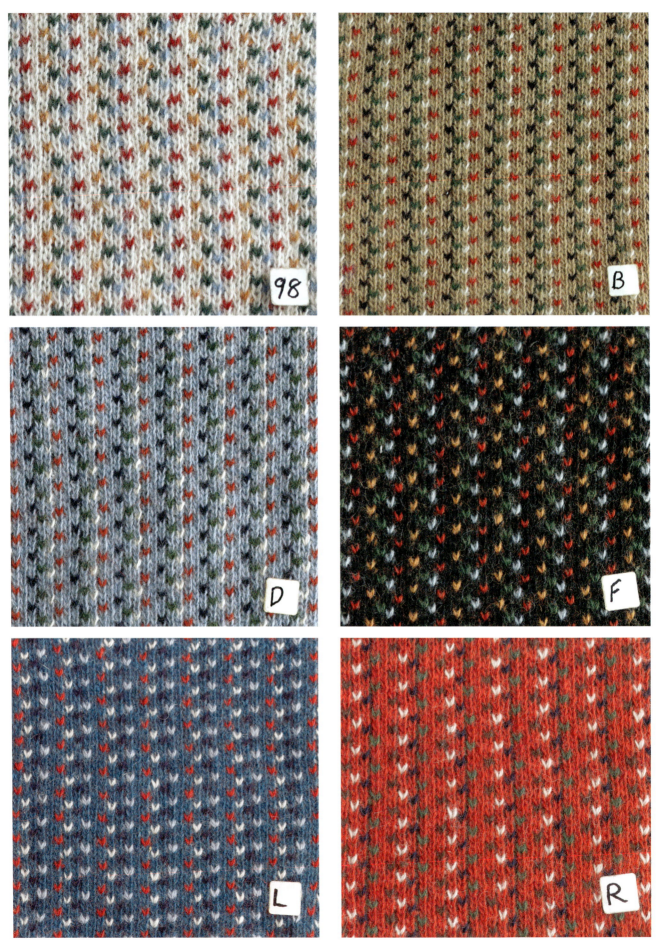

Knitted samples, most likely from the 1980s.

DESIGN
Dianna Walla

SKILL LEVEL
Experienced

SIZES
S (M, L)

FINISHED MEASUREMENTS
Hat: circumference, 19 (21, 23¾) in / 48 (53.5, 59) cm
Half-Gloves: circumference, 7 (7¾, 8½) in / 18 (19.5, 21.5) cm

MATERIALS
Yarn:
CYCA #2 (sport, baby) Rauma Finull PT2 (100% Norwegian wool, 191 yd/175 m / 50 g)

Yarn Colors and Amounts:
Suggestion 1:
Color 1: Black 436
Color 2: Charcoal Gray 414
Color 3: Dark Gray 405
Color 4: Gray 404
Color 5: Light gray 403

Suggestion 2:
Color 1: Petroleum 484
Color 2: Light Petroleum 483
Color 3: Light Peasant's Blue 451
Color 4: Light Turquoise 4705
Color 5: Mint Green 4887

Hat: 50 g of each color
Half-Gloves: 50 g of each color

Needles:
U. S. sizes 2.5 and 4 / 3 and 3.5 mm: 16 in / 40 cm circulars for cap or set of 5 dpn; dpns for mitts

GAUGE
28 sts x 29 rnds in stockinette pattern
on larger needles = 4 in / 10 cm.
Adjust needle size to obtain correct gauge if necessary.

HAT

With Color 1 and smaller circular, CO 136 (150, 166) sts. Join, being careful not to twist cast-on row; pm for beginning of rnd.

Work around in k1, p1 ribbing as follows:
3 rnds of (k1 Color 1, p1 Color 2).
3 rnds of (k1 Color 1, p1 Color 3).
3 rnds of (k1 Color 1, p1 Color 4).
3 rnds of (k1 Color 1, p1 Color 5).

Change to larger circular and knit 1 rnd with Color 1, *at the same time* decreasing 1 (0, 1) st = 135 (150, 165) sts rem.

Knit 1 rnd with Color 3, 1 rnd with Color 5, and 1 rnd with Color 1.

Now work in pattern following Chart 1. Work the repeat a total of 9 times in length. On the last rnd, pm after every 15th st. Change to dpn when sts no longer fit around circular.

Shape crown following Chart 2, decreasing before each marker as shown on chart.

FINISHING

Cut yarn and draw end through rem sts; tighten.
Weave in all ends neatly on WS.

HALF-GLOVES

With Color 1 and smaller dpn, CO 50 (56, 60) sts.
Divide sts onto dpn and join.

Work around in k1, p1 ribbing as follows:

2 rnds of (k1 Color 1, p1 Color 2).

2 rnds of (k1 Color 1, p1 Color 3).

2 rnds of (k1 Color 1, p1 Color 4).

2 rnds of (k1 Color 1, p1 Color 5).

Change to larger dpn and knit 1 rnd with Color 1, *at the same time* decreasing 1 (0, 1) st = 50 (55, 60) sts rem.

Knit 1 rnd with Color 3, 1 rnd with Color 5, and 1 rnd with Color 1.

Now work in pattern following Chart 1. Work the repeat a total of 6 times in length. On the next rnd, make thumbhole:

Left hand: Work following chart until 10 (10, 12) sts rem; place 10 (10, 12) sts on a holder for thumb and CO 10 (10, 12) sts new sts in pattern over the gap.

Right hand: Place first 10 (10, 12) sts on a holder for thumb and CO 10 (10, 12) sts new sts in pattern over the gap. Knit in pattern to end of rnd.

Continue following Chart 1.

Work pattern repeat 3 times in length above thumbhole.

Knit 1 rnd with Color 1, 1 rnd with Color 5, and 1 rnd with Color 3, 1 rnd with Color 1, increasing 0 (1, 0) sts = 50 (56, 60) sts on last rnd.

Change back to smaller dpn and work in ribbing as follows:

2 rnds of (k1 Color 1, p1 Color 5).

2 rnds of (k1 Color 1, p1 Color 4).

2 rnds of (k1 Color 1, p1 Color 3).

2 rnds of (k1 Color 1, p1 Color 2).

BO all sts with Color 1.

THUMB

Slip the 10 (10, 12) held sts to smaller dpn and, with Color 1, pick up and knit 10 (10, 12) sts across

top of thumbhole + 1 extra st on each side = 22 (22, 26) sts total.

With Color 1, work 5 rnds in k1, p1 ribbing.

BO all sts in ribbing.

FINISHING

Weave in all ends neatly on WS.

Chart 1

■ Color 1
▲ Color 2
• Color 3
⊠ Color 4
☐ Color 5

Chart 2

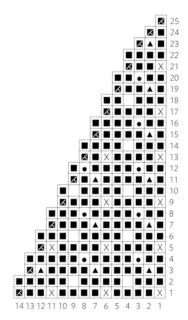

■ Color 1
▲ Color 2
• Color 3
⊠ Color 4
☐ Color 5

⊠ K2tog with Color 1

Klara

WOMEN'S PULLOVER WITH
COWL AND WRIST WARMERS

Klara is a lovely single-color pullover with a relief stitch pattern at the lower edge and an easy-going A-line silhouette. The sleeves are a little wide at the cuffs and the relief pattern of knit and purl stitches is repeated in the raglan shaping. This pattern, in production in the last half of the 1950s, might remind you of brickwork. The wrist warmers and cowl in the same relief pattern pair up with the sweater. The cowl can be worked in two sizes—long enough to wrap once or twice around the neck. A cool sweater for the younger generation!

Klara Delph (1911-1991) trained as a tailor and worked as a sample sewer for Salhus Tricotagefabrik. She also worked privately for director Clausen—repairing his undergarments was one of her sewing tasks. In the 1950s and 60s, she lived in an apartment in one of the worker residences right behind the factory.

Knitted samples from 1958.

DESIGN
Berit Løkken, Hillesvåg Ullvarefabrikk

SKILL LEVEL
Experienced

SIZES
S (M, L, XL, XXL)

FINISHED MEASUREMENTS
Pullover:
Chest: 36 (37½, 41¾, 45¾, 49¾) in /
91 (95, 106, 116, 126) cm
Total Length: as measured down center back, approx.
27½ (28, 28¼, 28¾, 29¼) in / 70 (71, 72, 73, 74) cm
Sleeve Length: 19¼ (19¾, 19¾, 20, 20) in /
49 (50, 50, 51, 51) cm
Cowl: 24½ in / 62 cm or 48¾ in / 124 cm around

MATERIALS
Yarn:
CYCA #1 (fingering) Hillesvåg Vilje lamullgarn
(lamb's wool yarn), (100% Norwegian wool,
410 yd/375 m / 100 g)
OR substitute with CYCA #1 (fingering) Hillesvåg Sølje
(100% Norwegian pelt sheep wool, 383 yd/350 m / 100 g)

Yarn Color and Amounts:
Pullover: Vilje Ochre 57404: 400 (450, 500, 550, 600) g
Cowl: Vilje Ochre 57404: 100 or 150 g
Wrist Warmers: Vilje Ochre 57404: 50 g

Needles:
U. S. size 1.5 / 2.5 mm: circular 32 in
/ 80 cm and set of 5 dpn.
U. S. size 2.5 / 3 mm: circulars 16 and 32 in / 40 and 80 cm
U. S. size 4 / 3.5 mm: circular 32 in / 80 cm.

GAUGE
25 sts x 32 rnds in stockinette on U. S. size 2.5
/ 3 mm needles = 4 x 4 in / 10 x 10 cm.
Adjust needle size to obtain correct gauge if necessary.

BODY
With U. S. 1.5 / 2.5 mm circular, CO 260 (270, 300, 320, 350) sts. Join, being careful not to twist cast-on row; pm for beginning of rnd. Work around in garter st (= alternate knit 1 rnd, purl 1 rnd = 1 ridge) for 3 ridges (= 6 rnds).

Change to U.S. 2.5 / 3 mm circular and continue in pattern following Chart 1 until body is approx. 7 (7, 8¼, 8¼, 8¼) in / 18 (18, 21, 21, 21) cm long. End with a complete repeat. Pm at each side with 130 (135, 150, 160, 175) sts each for front and back.

Continue in stockinette for ¾ in / 2 cm (all sizes).

Shape sides: *K4, ssk, knit until 6 sts before side marker, k2tog, k8, ssk, knit until 6 sts before next marker, k2tog, k4 = 4 sts decreased on rnd).*

Rep the decrease rnd every 9th (9th, 8th, 9th, 8th) rnd a total of 8 (8, 9, 8, 9) times = 228 (238, 264, 288, 314) sts rem.

Continue in stockinette without decreasing until body is 19¼ in / 49 cm long (all sizes).

BO 4 sts on each side of each side marker (= 8 sts bound off centered on each underarm).

Set body aside while you knit sleeves.

SLEEVES
With U. S. 1.5 / 2.5 mm dpn, CO 64 (66, 68, 70, 72) sts. Divide sts onto dpn and join. Work around in garter st (= alternate knit 1 rnd, purl 1 rnd = 1 ridge) for 3 ridges. Knit 3 rnds and then purl 2 rnds.

Change to U.S. 2.5 / 3 mm dpn and continue in stockinette.

On every 9th rnd, increase 1 st after first and 1 st before last st of rnd until there are 98 (100, 102, 104, 104) sts.

When sleeve is 19¼ (19¾, 19¾, 20, 20) in / 49 (50, 50, 51, 51) cm long, BO 8 sts centered on underarm.

Set sleeve aside while you knit the second sleeve the same way.

YOKE RAGLAN SHAPING

Arrange all the pieces on U.S. 2.5 / 3 mm circular as follows: rnd begins here—first sleeve, front, second sleeve, back = 392 (406, 436, 464, 490) sts total. Pm at each intersection of body and sleeve = 4 markers.

Begin raglan shaping as follows: K1, *k2tog, knit until 3 sts before next marker, ssk, k2*; rep * to * around, ending with k1 (= 8 sts decreased per rnd) = 384 (398, 428, 456, 482) sts.

Decrease the same way on every rnd a total of 4 (5, 6, 7, 8) times and then on every other rnd a total of 30 (30, 32, 34, 36) times, but work the 2 knit sts between decreases in pattern following Chart 2.

Now 120 (126, 132, 136, 138) sts rem. Pm at center back and work short rows to raise back neck as follows: Work until 10 sts past marker; turn, sl 1st st, work until 10 sts past marker on the other side. *Turn, work until 10 sts past first turn*; rep * to * until you've turned 4 times on each side (continue knitting in pattern inside the raglan lines as est). Now work around on all sts, decreasing evenly spaced around to 110 (116, 118, 120, 122) sts. Change to U. S. 1.5 / 2.5 mm circular and purl 2 rnds, knit 3 rnds and then work 3 garter ridges. BO.

FINISHING

Seam underarms. Weave in all ends neatly on WS.

Pat out sweater to finished measurements and lay on a damp towel. Cover with another damp towel and leave until pullover is completely dry. Or, lightly soak garment, spin out excess water in a spin dryer (centrifuge) and lay flat to dry.

COWL

With U. S. 2.5 / 3 mm circular, CO 50 sts. Work back and forth in pattern as follows: Work the first 5 sts in garter st (= knit all rows), work in pattern following Chart 1, and end with 5 sts garter st.

Continue in pattern until loop measures approx. 24½ in / 62 cm (for one wrap around neck) or 48¾ in / 124 cm (two wraps around neck). BO.

FINISHING

Seam short ends. Weave in all ends neatly on WS.

Lay cowl on a damp towel and pat out to finished measurements. Cover with another damp towel and leave until completely dry. Or, lightly soak cowl, spin out excess water in a spin dryer (centrifuge) and lay flat to dry.

WRIST WARMERS

With U. S. 1.5 / 2.5 mm dpn, CO 50 sts. Divide sts onto dpn and join. *Knit 1 rnd, purl 1 rnd* (= 1 garter ridge); rep * to * 2 more times = 3 garter ridges. Knit 3 rnds and then purl 2 rnds.

Change to U. S. 2.5 / 3 mm dpn and continue in pattern following Chart 1 until cuff is approx. 5¼ in / 13 cm long. End with a complete repeat.

Purl 2 rnds, knit 3 rnds, work 3 garter ridges. BO. Weave in all ends neatly on WS.

Chart 1   **Chart 2**

☒ Purl on RS, knit on WS
☐ Knit on RS, purl on WS

Komet

CHILDREN'S PULLOVER

The stripe pattern on these children's pullovers with raglan shaping was inspired by a pattern in use between 1910 and the 1920s. We borrowed its name from the coolest knitting machines in the museum: mint green 1960s sock-knitting machines that produce a sock in three minutes. The Komet machine was manufactured by Bentley Engineering Ltd in Leicester, which was a large producer of sock knitting machines in post-war England.

Knitted samples from the period 1910 to 1920.

DESIGN
Kristin Wiola Ødegård

SKILL LEVEL
Experienced

SIZES
2 (4, 6, 8, 10, 12) years

FINISHED MEASUREMENTS
Chest: 24½ (27¼, 30, 31½, 32¾, 34¼) in /
62 (69, 76, 80, 83, 87) cm
Total Length: 14½ (16¼, 17¾, 19, 20½, 21¾) in /
37 (41, 45, 48, 52, 55) cm
Sleeve Length: 9¾ (11, 12¼, 13½, 14½, 15¾) in /
25 (28, 31, 34, 37, 40) cm

MATERIALS
Yarn:
CYCA #3 (DK, light worsted) Sandnes Garn Per Gynt
(100% Norwegian wool, approx. 98 yd/91 m / 50 g)

Yarn Colors and Amounts:
Suggestion 1:
MC: Medium White 1002: 50 (50, 100, 100, 150, 150) g
CC1: Ochre 2035: 50 (50, 50, 100, 100, 100) g
CC2: Dusty Petroleum 7212: 50 (100, 100, 150, 150, 150) g
CC3: Sea Green 7024: 50 (100, 100, 150, 150, 150) g

Suggestion 2:
MC: Medium White 1002: 50 (50, 100, 100, 150, 150) g
CC1: Red 4228: 50 (50, 50, 100, 100, 100) g
CC2: Dusty Petroleum 7212: 50 (100, 100, 150, 150, 150) g
CC3: Sea Green 7024: 50 (100, 100, 150, 150, 150) g

Needles:
U. S. size 4 / 3.5 mm: circulars 16, 24, and
32 in / 40, 60, and 80 cm (32 in / 80 cm
only for 2 largest sizes); set of 5 dpn
U. S. size 2.5 / 3 mm: circular 16 in / 40 cm for neckband

GAUGE
22 sts x 20 rnds on larger needles = 4 x 4 in / 10 x 10 cm.
Adjust needle size to obtain correct gauge if necessary.

GARMENT CONSTRUCTION
All the pieces are knitted in the round on circular and double-pointed needles, before the pieces are joined with raglan shaping on the same circular needle.

RAGLAN SHAPING
Marker, k2tog, knit until 2 sts before next marker, k2tog tbl, marker; rep * to * at each intersection of sleeve and body on every other round (unless otherwise specified) = 8 sts decreased per round.

BODY
With CC1 and larger circular, CO 136 (152, 168, 176, 184, 192) sts. Join, being careful not to twist cast-on row; pm for beginning of rnd. Work around in k1, p1 ribbing for 1¼ (1¼, 1¼, 1½, 1½, 1½) in / 3 (3, 3, 4, 4, 4) cm.
Now work in pattern following chart until body measures approx. 9½ (10¾, 11¾, 13, 14¼, 15) in / 24 (27, 30, 33, 36, 38) cm.
End with a stripe in Dusty Petroleum or Sea Green.
Shape underarms:
BO 3 sts, k62 (70, 78, 82, 86, 90); BO 6 sts; k62 (70, 78, 82, 86, 90); BO 3 sts.
Set body aside while you knit the sleeves.

SLEEVES
With CC1 and larger dpn, CO 36 (36, 40, 40, 44, 44) sts. Divide sts onto dpn and join.
Work around in k1, p1 ribbing for 1¼ (1¼, 1¼, 1½, 1½, 1½) in / 3 (3, 3, 4, 4, 4) cm.

Note: Measure stripes on the body to determine which color stripe should begin sleeve so that sleeve and body will match at underarms.

Work in pattern following the chart. *At the same time*, increase 2 sts centered on underarm every ¾ in / 2 cm until there are a total of 56 (60, 64, 68, 72, 72) sts.

When sleeve is approx. 9¾ (11, 12¼, 13½, 14½, 15¾) in / 25 (28, 31, 34, 37, 40) cm long, end at same place in stripe sequence as on body.

BO 6 sts centered on underarm. Set sleeve aside while you knit second sleeve the same way.

YOKE WITH RAGLAN SHAPING

Arrange all the pieces larger circular = 224 (248, 272, 288, 304, 312) sts total. Pm at each intersection of body and sleeve = 4 markers.

Work stripe sequence as est and, *at the same time*, shape raglan.

Work raglan shaping as described above on *every* rnd 6 (6, 7, 7, 8, 9) times.

Now decrease as est on *every other rnd* 11 (13, 15, 17, 18, 18) times = 88 (96, 96, 96, 96, 96) sts rem.

Work the 5 last chart rows (see note to right of chart), change to smaller circular and decrease 16 (16, 14, 12, 10, 8) sts evenly spaced around = 72 (80, 82, 84, 86, 88) sts rem.

With CC1, work around in k1, p1 ribbing for 2½ (2½, 2½, 3¼, 3¼, 3¼) in / 6 (6, 6, 8, 8, 8) cm. BO loosely knitwise.

Fold neckband in half and sew down edge on WS with overhand stitches.

FINISHING

Seam underarms. Weave in all ends neatly on WS.

Lay sweater on a damp towel and pat out to finished measurements. Cover with another damp towel and leave until pullover is completely dry. Or, lightly soak garment, spin out excess water in a spin dryer (centrifuge) and lay flat to dry.

Chart

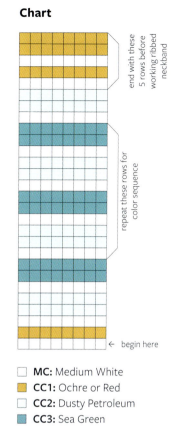

end with these 5 rows before working ribbed neckband

repeat these rows for color sequence

← begin here

- ☐ **MC:** Medium White
- ☐ **CC1:** Ochre or Red
- ☐ **CC2:** Dusty Petroleum
- ☐ **CC3:** Sea Green

Cobra SKIRT

This is another stripe pattern from the early twentieth century, which has found new life on the edge of an A-line black skirt. The pattern really stands out with strongly contrasting colors—it's almost as if the white and yellow stripes glow against the background. The name stems from a Salhus Tricotagefabrik brand for sportswear in the 1980s, but also, of course, the cobra snake, which can also be black with yellow stripes.

The skirt has elastic knitted together with the yarn in the ribbed top edge. It's knittd in the round from the top down, with ribbing followed by a stockinette section with increases evenly spaced between markers.

Knitted samples from the period 1910 to 1920.

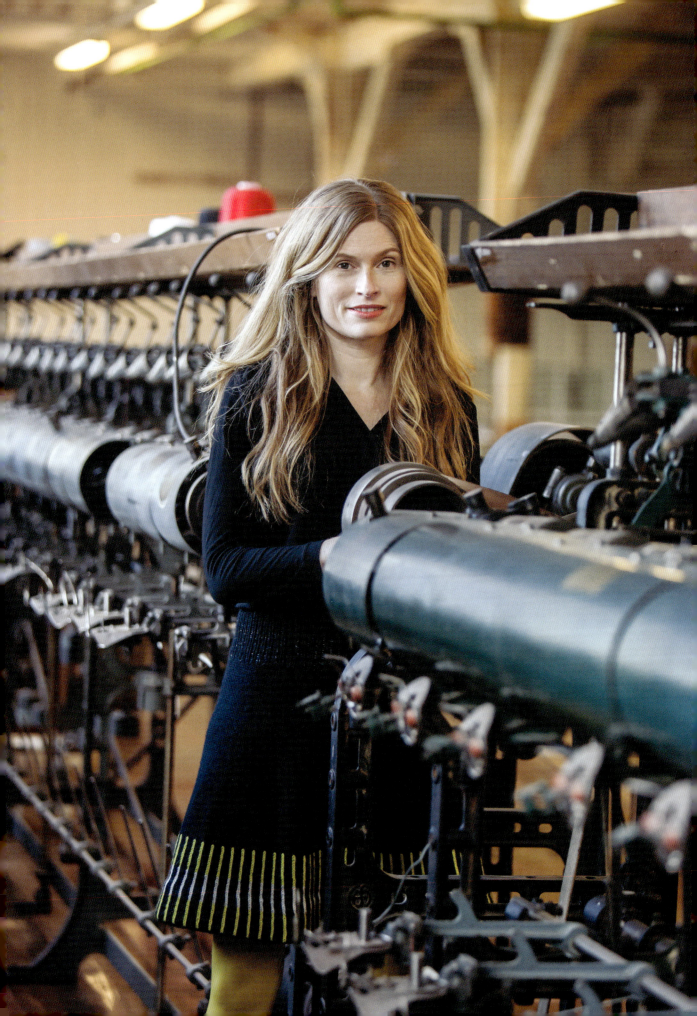

DESIGN
Birte Sandvik and Margareth Sandvik

SKILL LEVEL
Experienced

SIZES
XS (S, M, L, XL)

FINISHED MEASUREMENTS
Total Length: including ribbing, 18¼ (19, 20, 22, 24) in / 46 (48.5, 51, 56, 61) cm
Width: approx. measurement, as measured beneath ribbing, 24 (25½, 27½, 29, 32½) in / 61 (65, 70, 75, 80) cm

Note: All knitted garments are very elastic. A good tip is to place all the sts on a long strand of yarn and try on the skirt to make sure the width of the ribbing fits well before you continue to the total length.

MATERIALS
Yarn:
CYCA #2 (sport, baby) Rauma Garn Tumi (50% alpaca, 50% wool, 142 yd/130 m / 50 g)

Yarn Colors and Amounts:
MC: Black SFN50: 250 (250, 250, 250, 300) g
CC1: White SFN10 2035: 50 (50, 50, 50, 50) g
CC2: Yellow B141: 50 (50, 50, 50, 50) g

Notions:
Knitting-in elastic, transparent (available from prym.com)

Needles:
U. S. size 4 / 3.5 mm: circulars 16, 24, and 32 in / 40, 60, and 80 cm

GAUGE
24 sts = 4 in / 10 cm.
Adjust needle size to obtain correct gauge if necessary.

KNITTING TIPS
For a more even pattern when knitting with two strands held at the same time over your index finger (continental method), work as follows: Place the non-dominant color of the repeat nearest you on your index finger. For example, first repeat: place the yellow lower down on your finger, with black on top, near the fingernail. Work with yarns held in that sequence for 12 rounds. Replace yellow with white, and hold white lower down and black higher. Work 12 rounds and then replace white with yellow.

SKIRT
With 16 in / 40 cm circular and Black Tumi and elastic thread held together, CO 118 (128, 140, 150, 162) sts. Join, being careful not to twist cast-on row; pm for beginning of rnd.

Work around in k1, p1 ribbing for 4¾ in / 12 cm. Cut elastic.

Continue with Black only and work around in stockinette, *at the same time* increasing 30 sts evenly spaced around on the 1st rnd.

Knit 10 rnds with Black. Now place 9 markers evenly spaced around, increasing 1 st on each side of each marker. Work 8 (9, 10, 12, 14) rnds without increasing.

Knit 1 rnd, increasing 1 st on each side of each marker. Work 8 (9, 10, 12, 14) rnds without increasing.

Repeat * to * until you've increased a total of 8 times = 292 (302, 314, 324, 336) sts.

Knit 1 rnd with Black.

Note: For sizes M and L: Knit 1 rnd Black, increasing 2 sts evenly spaced around so the stitch count is a multiple of 4.

Now begin working from the chart.
K3 Black, k1 Yellow, k3 Black, k1 Yellow; rep * to * around.
Work sequence above 12 times total and then switch Yellow to White.
K3 Black, k1 White, k3 Black, k1 White; rep * to * around.

Work sequence above 12 times total and then switch
  White to Yellow.
K3 Black, k1 Yellow, k3 Black, k1 Yellow*; rep * to *
  around.
Work sequence above 12 times total.
After completing charted rows, knit 1 rnd Black.
Purl 1 rnd (foldline) with Black and then continue in
  stockinette st for 2½ in / 6 cm for facing.
BO loosely.

FINISHING

Sew down hem facing on WS.
Weave in all ends neatly on WS.

Note: Do *not* steam press the ribbing. This way, it
  won't lose its elasticity—and you won't melt the
  elastic thread.

Lay a damp pressing cloth over the skirt. Gently
  steam press skirt until it is damp. Leave flat until
  completely dry.

Chart

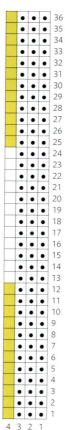

- ⊡ **MC:** Black
- ☐ **CC1:** White
- 🟨 **CC2:** Yellow

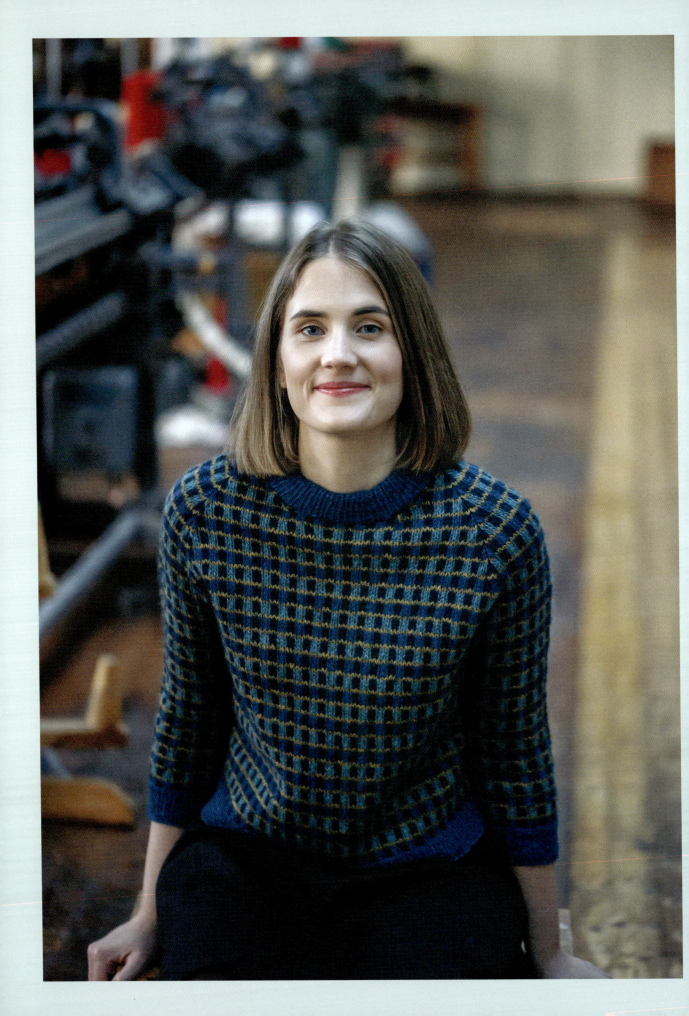

Opal Women's Pullover

Opal is a pretty women's pullover with a pattern of crisscrossing stripes. The three-quarter-length sleeves and cropped body create a fine retro silhouette. The pattern is derived from knitted samples from the 1980s and is knitted here in blue shades of Tinde pelt wool yarn, with yellow vertical stripes. The name is taken from one of the most popular undergarment brands at Salhus Tricotagefabrik and from the colorful opal stone.

Each of these brands of cotton undergarments were made with "double knit" interlock fabric and, while Krone Opal took over from Krone Maco, it was never as iconic as "Maco."

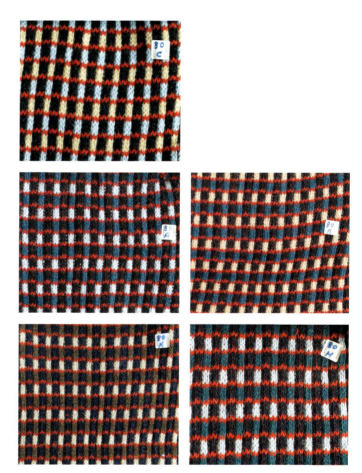

Knitted samples, probably from the 1980s.

Color Suggestion 2

DESIGN
Diana Walla

SKILL LEVEL
Experienced

SIZES
XS (S, M, L, XL)

FINISHED MEASUREMENTS
Chest: 32¼ (36¼, 39½, 45¼, 49¼) in /
82 (92, 100, 115, 125) cm
Total Length: as measured down center front,
18½ (19¾, 21, 22) in / 47 (50, 53, 56) cm
Sleeve Length: 13 (13, 13, 13½, 13½) in /
33 (33, 33, 34.5, 34.5) cm

MATERIALS
Yarn:

CYCA #3 (DK, light worsted) Hillesvåg Tinde pelsullgarn
(100% Norwegian pelt sheep wool, 284 yd/260 m / 100 g)

Yarn Colors and Amounts:
Suggestion 1:
Color 1: Petroleum 652105: 150 (150, 150, 200, 200) g
Color 2: Navy Blue 652133: 200 (250, 250, 300, 350) g
Color 3: Light Turquoise 652130: 100 (100, 150, 150, 150) g
Color 4: Red-Yellow 652122: 50 (50, 50, 50, 50) g

Suggestion 2:
Color 1: Burgundy 652104: 150 (150, 150, 200, 200) g
Color 2: Burgundy-Violet 652131: 200 (250, 250, 300, 350) g
Color 3: Cognac 652103: 100 (100, 150, 150, 150) g
Color 4: Red-Yellow 652122: 50 (50, 50, 50, 50) g

Needles:
U. S. sizes 4 and 6 / 3.5 and 4 mm: circulars 16 and 32 in /
40 and 80 cm; sets of 5 dpn or long Magic Loop circulars—
or needles for the method you prefer for knitting sleeves

GAUGE
22 sts x 28 rnds in pattern on larger
needles = 4 x 4 in / 10 x 10 cm.
Adjust needle size to obtain correct gauge if necessary.

BODY

With Color 1 and smaller long circular, CO 180 (200, 220, 252, 276) sts. Join, being careful not to twist cast-on row; pm for beginning of rnd.

Work around in k1, p1 ribbing for 1½ in / 4 cm. Pm at each side with 90 (100, 110, 126, 138) sts each for front and back.

Change to larger circular and knit around in pattern following Chart 1 until body measures approx. 11½ (11¾, 12¼, 12¾, 13) in / 29 (30, 31, 32, 33) cm, ending with a complete repeat.

BO 8 (10, 12, 14, 16) sts centered at each side for underarm = BO 4 (5, 6, 7, 8) sts on each side of each side marker.

Set body aside while you knit sleeves.

SLEEVES

With Color 1 and smaller dpn, or the needle style you prefer for small circumferences, CO 48 (52, 56, 56, 60) sts. Divide sts onto dpn if using and join; pm for beginning of rnd at center of underarm.

Work around in k1, p1 ribbing for 2 in / 5 cm.

Change to larger dpn and knit around in pattern following Chart 1. When sleeve is 4 in / 10 cm long, begin shaping: increase 1 st on each side of marker. Increase the same way every 7th (7th, 8th, 8th, 9th) rnd 5 (7, 7, 11, 11) times more = 60 (68, 72, 80, 84) sts.

Continue in pattern until sleeve is 13 (13, 13, 13½, 13½) in / 33 (33, 33, 34.5, 34.5) cm long or desired length. End with a complete repeat.

BO 8 (10, 12, 14, 16) sts centered on underarm = BO 4 (5, 6, 7, 8) sts on each side of marker. Set sleeve aside while you knit the second sleeve the same way.

RAGLAN SHAPING

Arrange body and sleeves on larger circular = 268 (296, 316, 356, 380) sts total.

Pm at each intersection of body and sleeve. The rnd now begins at the left sleeve.

Work following the chart for the body and sleeves. *At the same time*, decrease for raglan on every other rnd.

K2tog, knit until 2 sts before next marker, sl 1, k1, psso (or ssk), sl m; rep * to * around.

Decrease the same way on every other rnd a total of 16 (17, 18, 20, 20) times = 140 (160, 172, 196, 220) sts rem.

NECK SHAPING

See Chart 2 for your size.

Rnd 1: Continue in pattern following Chart 1. Knit sts of left sleeve, k18 (19, 21, 25, 30) sts on front, BO the next 14 (18, 20, 22, 22) sts, knit to end of rnd = 126 (142, 152, 174, 198) sts rem.

Rnd 2: K2tog, knit until 2 sts before marker, ssk, k2tog. Knit until 3 sts before front neck, ssk, k1, pm, CO 5 new sts for steek, pm, k1, *k2tog, knit until 2 sts before marker ssk; rep from * to end of rnd = 10 sts decreased.

PART 1

Rnd 3: Work as est until 3 sts before steek marker, ssk, k1, knit steek sts, k1, k2tog, knit to end of rnd = 2 sts decreased.

Rnd 4: K2tog, knit until 2 sts before marker, ssk, k2tog. Knit until 3 sts before marker, ssk, k1, work steek sts, k1, *k2tog, knit until 2 sts before marker, ssk; rep from * to end of rnd = 10 sts decreased.

Rep Rnds 3-4 once more.

PART 2

Next Rnd: Work all sts in pattern following Chart 1.

Next Rnd: K2tog, knit until 2 sts before marker, ssk, k2tog. Knit until 3 sts before marker, ssk, k1, work steek sts, k1, *k2tog, knit until 2 sts before marker, ssk; rep from * to end of rnd = 10 sts decreased.

Rep these 2 rnds 2 (2, 3,4, 4) more times.

Only for sizes XS, S, and M:

Next Rnd: Work all sts in pattern following Chart 1.

Next Rnd: Decrease 1 st at each side of each raglan marker and decrease 1 st on each side of neck = 10 sts decreased.

Next 2 rnds—only for size XS:

Next Rnd: Work around as est.

Next Rnd: Decrease 1 st at each side of each raglan marker = 8 sts decreased.

Next 2 rnds—only for size S:

Next Rnd: Work around following Chart 1.

Next Rnd: Decrease 2 sts between raglan marker on front and neck edge, decrease 1 st at each side of all other raglan markers = 10 sts decreased.

PART 3

Only for sizes XS and S:

Next Rnd: Work around following Chart 1.

Next Rnd: Decrease 1 st on each side of neck, decrease 1 st at raglan markers as shown at all other places on chart = 6 sts decreased.

Only for sizes M, L, and XL:

Next Rnd: Work around following Chart 1.

Next Rnd: Decrease 1 st each side of each raglan marker as shown on chart, but only at raglan markers = 8 sts decreased.

Rep these 2 rnds once more.

All sizes:

Work 1 rnd following pattern chart.

BO all sts.

NECKBAND

If you are knitting with Norwegian wool that isn't superwash, you can reinforce the steek by crocheting a row of sc on each side of center steek st, or machine-stitching two lines on each side of steek center st. If you are knitting with another yarn type or superwash wool, machine-stitch 2 lines on each side of center steek st. Carefully cut steek open up center st.

With smaller circular and Color 1, pick up and knit 3 sts for every 4 sts/rows around neck. The stitch count must be a multiple of 2.

Work around in k1, p1 ribbing for 3¼ in / 8 cm. BO in ribbing. Fold neckband in half and sew down edge loosely to WS.

Chart 1

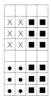

- ● Color 1: Petroleum
- ■ Color 2: Navy Blue
- ☒ Color 3: Light Turquoise
- ☐ Color 4: Red-Yellow

- ■ Decreases, Part 2
- ■ Decreases, Part 3

- ╱ K2tog
- ╲ Ssk or sl 1, k1, psso
- ⋏ K3tog

Chart 2 (size XS)

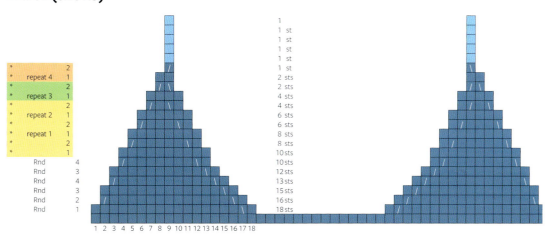

Chart 2 (size M)

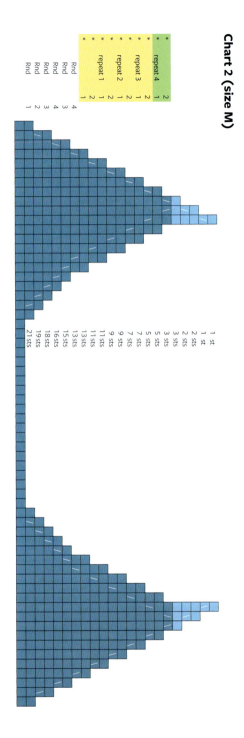

repeat 4	2	*
repeat 3	1	*
repeat 2	2	*
repeat 1	1	*
	2	*
	1	*
	2	*
	1	*
Rnd	4	
Rnd	3	
Rnd	2	
Rnd	1	

Chart 2 (size S)

154

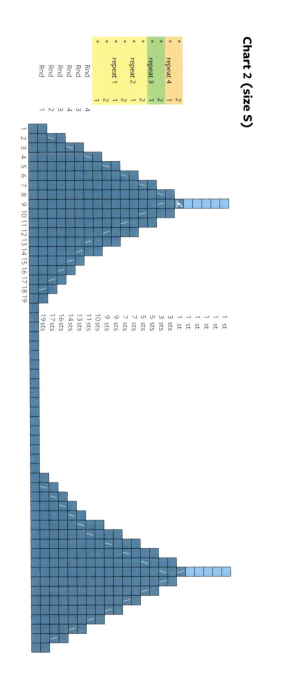

repeat 4	2	*
repeat 3	1	*
repeat 2	2	*
repeat 1	1	*
	2	*
	1	*
	2	*
	1	*
Rnd	4	
Rnd	3	
Rnd	2	
Rnd	1	

Chart 2 (size XL)

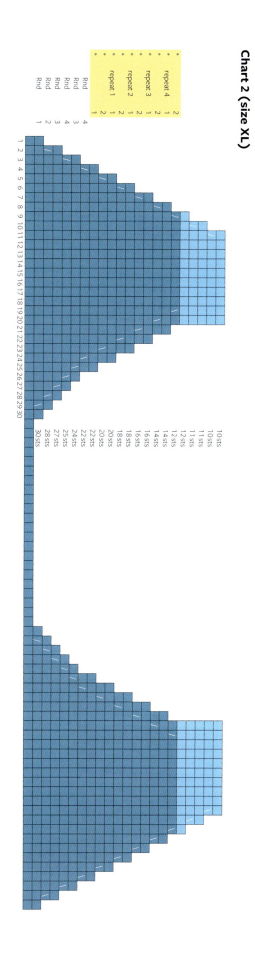

* repeat 4	2 / 1
* repeat 3	2 / 1
* repeat 2	2 / 1
* repeat 1	2 / 1
Rnd	4
Rnd	3
Rnd	2
Rnd	1

Row numbers: 1 2 3 4 5 6 7 8 9 10 11 12 13 14 15 16 17 18 19 20 21 22 23 24 25 26 27 28 29 30

10 sts
10 sts
11 sts
11 sts
12 sts
12 sts
14 sts
14 sts
16 sts
16 sts
18 sts
18 sts
20 sts
20 sts
22 sts
22 sts
24 sts
25 sts
27 sts
28 sts
30 sts

Chart 2 (size L)

* repeat 4	2 / 1
* repeat 3	2 / 1
* repeat 2	2 / 1
* repeat 1	2 / 1
Rnd	4
Rnd	3
Rnd	2
Rnd	1

Row numbers: 1 2 3 4 5 6 7 8 9 10 11 12 13 14 15 16 17 18 19 20 21 22 23 24 25

5 sts
5 sts
6 sts
6 sts
7 sts
7 sts
9 sts
9 sts
11 sts
11 sts
13 sts
13 sts
15 sts
15 sts
17 sts
17 sts
19 sts
20 sts
22 sts
23 sts
25 sts

Asjur

UNISEX SPORTS PULLOVER

We designed this pullover inspired by a stripe pattern from the period 1910-1920. The motif is similar to the pattern *bakkin og grøvin* ("ridge and ditch") in Hans M. Debes' collection of Faroese knitting motifs, but with longer stripes. At Salhus Tricotagefabrik, the pattern seems to have been used as a panel; in the Faroe Islands, it's an all-over design for fishermen's sweaters.

Here you can see the pattern on a unisex sports sweater with a boat neck. The pattern panel is worked in two-color stranded stockinette, and the stripes are reflected in the relief stitch pattern on the pullover. A light main color was chosen to highlight the relief stitch structure. Asjur was an undergarment brand at Salhus Tricotagefabrik from the 1930s onwards.

À *jour* in French means "up-to-date." With wool underclothing from Salhus, you would be up-to-date at the height of the 1930s. The knitted samples to the right are from the decade prior.

Knitted samples, from the period 1910-1920.

Color Suggestion 1

Color Suggestion 2

DESIGN
Kristin Wiola Ødegård

SKILL LEVEL
Experienced

SIZES
S (M, L, XL, XXL)

FINISHED MEASUREMENTS
Chest: 34¾ (38¼, 41¾, 45¼, 48¾) in /
88 (97, 106, 115, 124) cm
Total Length: 25¼ (27½, 28¾, 30¼, 31) in /
64 (70, 73, 77, 79) cm
Sleeve Length: 18½ (19¾, 20½, 21¼) in /
47 (49, 50, 52, 54) cm

MATERIALS
Yarn:

CYCA #2 (sport, baby) Rauma Finull PT2 (100%
Norwegian wool, 191 yd/175 m / 50 g)

Yarn Colors and Amounts:
Suggestion 1:

MC: Light Gray 403: 400 (450, 500, 500, 550) g
CC1: Light Heather 473: 50 (50, 50, 50, 50) g
CC2: Heather 427: 50 (50, 50, 50, 50) g

Suggestion 2:

MC: Light Beige Heather 4078: 400 (450, 500, 500, 550) g
CC1: Dark Petroleum 438: 50 (50, 50, 50, 50) g
CC2: Blue-Gray 4287: 50 (50, 50, 50, 50) g

Needles:
U. S. size 2.5 / 3 mm: circulars 16 and
32 in / 40 and 80 cm; set of 5 dpn

GAUGE
27 sts x 30 rnds in pattern = 4 x 4 in / 10 x 10 cm.
Adjust needle size to obtain correct gauge if necessary.

RIBBING
Ribbing and stripe sequence at lower edges of body
and sleeves:
8 rnds MC
2 rnds CC1
4 rnds MC
2 rnds CC2
4 rnds MC
2 rnds CC1
1 rnd MC

BODY
With MC and long circular, CO 224 (248, 272, 296,
320) sts. Join, being careful not to twist cast-on
row; pm for beginning of rnd. Work ribbing and
stripe sequence described above.
Knit 1 rnd, *at the same time* increasing 16 sts evenly
spaced around = 240 (264, 288, 312, 336) sts.
Work in pattern following Chart 1 until body
measures 13½ (14½, 15¾, 16½, 17¼) in / 34
(37, 40, 42, 44) cm.
Work in pattern following Chart 2 (approx. 2¾ in /
7 cm). On last row of Chart 2, BO 9 (9, 11, 13,
15) sts centered at each side for underarm. Body
should now measure approx. 16¼ (17¼, 18½,
19¼, 20) in / 41 (44, 47, 49, 51) cm.
Now separate to work front and back separately =
111 (123, 133, 143, 153) sts each.

FRONT

Work back and forth in pattern following Chart 1 and, *at the same time*, at each armhole edge, BO 2, 2, 1, 1 sts at beginning of row (all sizes) = 6 sts bound off at each side = 99 (111, 121, 131, 141) sts rem.

When front is 1½ (1½, 2, 2, 2) in / 4 (4, 5, 5, 5) cm shorter than total length, BO the center 31 (33, 33, 35, 35) sts for neck.

Now work right and left sides of neck separately = 34 (39, 44, 48, 53) sts on each side.

Right side: Continue binding off at neck edge on every other row 3, 2, 2, 1 sts (all sizes) = 8 sts bound off.

Continue in pattern without further shaping until piece measures total length. BO rem sts for shoulder.

Left side: Work as for right side, reversing shaping to correspond.

BACK

Work back and forth in pattern following Chart 1 and, *at the same time*, at each armhole edge, BO 2, 2, 1, 1 sts at beginning of row (all sizes) = 6 sts bound off at each side = 99 (111, 121, 131, 141) sts rem.

Continue in pattern without further shaping until piece measures total length. BO rem sts.

SLEEVES

With MC and dpn, CO 50 (54, 54, 56, 58) sts. Divide sts onto dpn and join. Work Ribbing and Stripe sequence described above.

Knit 1 rnd, *at the same time* increasing 8 sts evenly spaced around = 58 (62, 62, 64, 66) sts.

Work in pattern following Chart 1. Count out from arrow for center of sleeve to determine beginning st for your size. Make sure pattern is centered on sleeve.

Note: Always purl the last st of rnd = center of underarm.

Every ¾ in / 2 cm, increase 1 st on each side of center purl st until there are 90 (100, 110, 112, 116) sts. Continue increasing as est, and, *at the same time*, work in pattern following Chart 2 until sleeve is 15¾ (16½, 17, 17¾, 18½) in / 40 (42, 43, 45, 47) cm long.

After completing Chart 2, the sleeve should measure 18½ (19¾, 20½, 21¼) in / 47 (49, 50, 52, 54) cm. BO 9 (9, 11, 13, 15) sts centered on underarm. Now begin working back and forth.

At the beginning of every row, BO 2, 2, 1, 1 (all sizes). BO 1 st at each side every 4th row until piece is 4¾ in / 12 cm above underarm.

BO rem sleeve sts loosely.

Make the second sleeve the same way.

FINISHING

Join shoulders. Attach sleeves.

NECKBAND

With MC and short circular, pick up and knit 100 (100, 108, 112, 120) sts around neck. Work around in k1, p1 ribbing for 1¼ (1¼, 1½, 1½, 1½) in / 3 (3, 4, 4, 4) cm.

BO loosely in ribbing.

Weave in all ends neatly on WS.

Chart 1

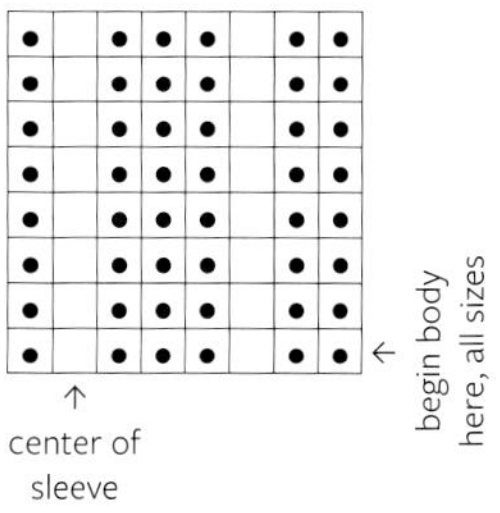

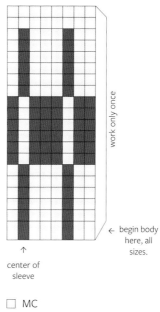

↑
center of
sleeve

← begin body
here, all sizes

Main Color

⊙ purl on RS, knit on WS
☐ knit on RS, purl on WS

Chart 2

↑
center of
sleeve

work only once

← begin body
here, all
sizes.

☐ MC
■ CC1

Factory Scarf

The same stripe pattern as for the previous sweater appears here in a single-color scarf. The scarf is a must for guests in big drafty industrial buildings, or as protection in chilly weather. The pattern from the Asjur pullover is worked in one color with knit and purl stitches for a simple and fine relief surface. If you want, you can use leftover yarns in various colors for the fringe—or just use one color for the entire project.

DESIGN
Kristin Wiola Ødegård

SKILL LEVEL
Easy

FINISHED MEASUREMENTS
Width: approx. 8 in / 20 cm
Length: approx. 78¾ in / 200 cm

MATERIALS
Yarn:
CYCA #1 (fingering) Hillesvåg Sølje (100% Norwegian pelt sheep wool, 383 yd/350 m / 100 g)

Yarn Color and Amount:
Suggestion 1:
Light Turquoise 2130: 200 g

Suggestion 2:
Natural Gray 2115: 200 g

Assorted colors of leftover yarn for fringe—or use the same yarn as for scarf

Needles:
U. S. size 2.5 / 3 mm: straight or circular 16 in / 40 cm

Crochet Hook:
U. S. size D-3 / 3 mm or slightly larger, for fringe

GAUGE
25 sts in pattern = 4 in / 10 cm.
Adjust needle size to obtain correct gauge if necessary.

EDGE STITCHES
Always slip the first st of the row knitwise and purl the last st.

SCARF
With straight or circular needle, CO 51 sts. Work back and forth following chart. Don't forget the edge sts (see above).
When scarf is approx. 78¾ in / 200 cm long or desired length, repeat the first 6 rows of the chart so the ends will match.

FINISHING
Weave in all ends neatly on WS. Make the fringe as described below. Gently steam press scarf under a damp pressing cloth.

FRINGE
Cut the desired number of strands about 11¾ in / 30 cm long and fold them to make a loop (see drawings).
Draw groups of strands through every other knit stitch at each end of the scarf, beginning with the knit stitch at outer edge.
Pull the strands through loop and tighten.

The yarn will soften up considerably after washing.

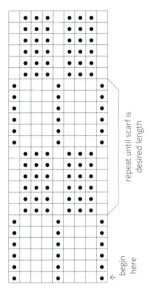

repeat until scarf is desired length

← begin here

☐ knit on RS, purl on WS
⦿ purl on RS, knit on WS

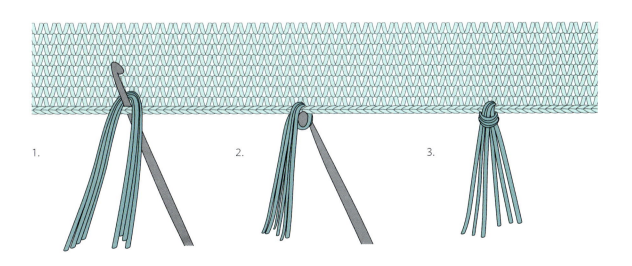

1.

2.

3.

Stay in style with the Asjur dress and matching double-layer scarf. The dress has a slight swing skirt and a three-color pattern panel plus pink for a contrast color on the sleeve edges. The scarf is knitted in the round, and the ends sewn or Kitchener stitched together. This stripe pattern probably originated early in the twentieth century.

DESIGN

Birte Sandvik and Margareth Sandvik

SKILL LEVEL

Experienced

SIZES

XS (S, M, L, XL)

FINISHED MEASUREMENTS

Chest: as measured with sleeves set in, 37 (39¾, 42½, 45¼, 48) in / 94 (101, 108, 115, 122) cm

Total Length: 30¾ in / 78 cm (all sizes)

Sleeve Length: 17¾ in / 45 cm (all sizes)

MATERIALS

Yarn:

CYCA #3 (DK, light worsted) Sandnes Garn Alpakka (100% alpaca, 120 yd/110 m / 50 g)

Yarn Colors and Amounts:

Color 1: Putty 1015: 500 (550, 550, 600, 650) g
Color 2: Burnt Orange 3355: 50 (50, 50, 50, 50) g
Color 3: Dusty Petroleum 7212: 50 (50, 50, 50, 50) g
Color 4: Ochre 2035: 50 (50, 50, 50, 50) g
Color 5: Pink 4715: 50 (50, 50, 50, 50) g

Needles:

U. S. size 4 / 3.5 mm: circulars 16 and 32 in / 40 and 80 cm; set of 5 dpn

GAUGE

24 sts = 4 in / 10 cm.

Adjust needle size to obtain correct gauge if necessary.

Knitting Tips:

For a more even pattern when knitting with two strands held at the same time over your index finger (continental method), work as follows: Place the non-dominant color of the repeat nearest you on your index finger. For example, first repeat: place the Burnt Orange lower down on your finger, with Putty on top, near the fingernail. Work with yarns held in that sequence for 5 rounds. For the next 6 rounds, hold Putty lower down your index finger and Burnt Orange near your nail. Change back to the original order for the last 5 rounds of pattern.

FRONT AND BACK

The front and back are worked as one piece, knitted in the round up to the underarms where the pieces are then separated.

Note: Please read through the next section before you knit so you will understand how the dress is shaped.

With Color 1 and long circular, CO 224 (240, 256, 276, 300) sts. Join, being careful not to twist cast-on row; pm for beginning of rnd. Knit around in stockinette for 1½ in / 4 cm.

Knit 1 eyelet rnd: (K2tog, yo) around and then continue in stockinette.

When body measures 7 in / 18 cm above eyelet rnd, begin pattern with Color 2 following the chart. If you want a longer dress, work extra rnds of stockinette before beginning pattern.

All of the decreases are in the Putty section where there is no patterning.

After the first pattern panel, pm at each side with the same number of sts each for front and back. On each side of this point, there is 1 st that is always knit, before and after the decreases.

Decrease 2 sts on each side as follows: ssk, k2, k2tog = 4 sts decreased per round. In the Putty section between the panels, decrease the same way 2 times = decrease a total of 8 sts between panels 1 and 2 and 8 sts between panels 2 and 3, a total of 16 sts decreased.

Knit 16 rnds in Color 1 after the first pattern panel and, *at the same time*, decrease as described above. Work pattern panel in Color 3. Knit 16 rnds in Color 1 and then work decrease rnd. Work pattern panel with Color 4.

Directly after the 3rd panel, decrease again = 208 (224, 240, 260, 284) sts rem.

Now, in addition to decreasing at the sides, decrease 2 times on the front and 2 times on the back = a total of 6 times in the round. In other words, determine 2 points for decreasing on both front and back. Divide the stitch count on front and stitch count on back by 3. Pm each of those points, with 2 markers each on front and back; make sure there are the same number of sts between each marker. Now you will begin decreasing as est at the sides, ssk, k2, k2tog. That means that you decrease 4 sts each on front and back, in addition to the 2 sts at each side (= 12 sts decreased per round).

Rep this sequence 4 times, first with 2 in / 5 cm between decrease rnds, then 1½ in / 4 cm, next, 1¼ in / 3 cm = 160 (176, 192, 212, 236) sts rem.

Knit to desired length. The size M dress shown in the photos is 24½ in / 62 cm long from the eyelet rnd up to the underarms.

At underarms, divide for front and back and work each side separately, working back and forth in stockinette (knit on RS, purl on WS). Begin by working back up to the shoulders = total length = 30¾ in / 78 cm.

Place the center 20 sts on a holder for neck and work each side separately. BO 1 st at neck edge 6 times. Place rem sts on a holder. Work opposite side of neck the same way. Reversing shaping to match.

Work front as for back.

Set body aside while you knit sleeves.

SLEEVES

With Color 5 and dpn, CO 70 sts (all sizes). Divide sts onto dpn and join. Work around in stockinette for 1½, in / 4 cm.

Knit 1 eyelet rnd: (K2tog, yo) around and then continue in stockinette with Color 5 for another 1½ in / 4 cm.

Change to Color 1. For a slight trumpet shape on the sleeve, decrease 2 sts centered on underarm to angle sleeve a little inwards.

Repeat this decrease 3 times for a total of 6 sts decreased.

If you want straight sleeves without the trumpet shaping, work sleeves without any decreases.

When sleeve is 6 in / 15 cm long, work pattern panel with Color 4. Continue in stockinette until sleeve is 17¾ in / 45 cm long. BO loosely.

FINISHING

Pin sleeves into armholes to make sure they fit. If not, adjust length of front and back. For example, if the sleeves are too wide at the top, add a few rows each to front and back.

Join shoulders with Kitchener st.

Attach sleeves with back stitch, RS to RS.

NECKBAND

With Color 1 and short circular, pick up the 20 sts at center front and back necks + 16 sts on each side = 72 total.

Knit 5 rnds, then work an eyelet rnd, knit 5 more rnds and then BO loosely.

Fold neckband along eyelet rnd and sew facing down on WS using same yarn and color as for knitting.

Weave in all ends neatly on WS.

Chart

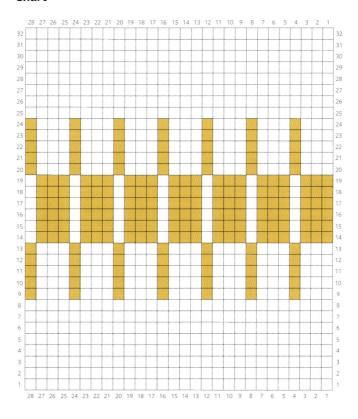

□ Color 1

▨ Colors 2, 3, 4, 5

DESIGN
Birte Sandvik and Margareth Sandvik

SKILL LEVEL
Experienced

FINISHED MEASUREMENTS
Length: approx. 71 in / 180 cm
Width: approx. 11¾ in / 30 cm

MATERIALS
Yarn:

CYCA #3 (DK, light worsted) Sandnes Garn
Alpakka (100% alpaca, 120 yd/110 m / 50 g)

Yarn Color and Amounts:

MC: Putty 1015: 350 g
CC1: Dusty Petroleum 7212: 50 g
CC2: Ochre 2035: 50 g
CC3: Burnt Orange 3355: 50 g
CC4: Pink 4715: 50 g

Needles:

U. S. size 4 / 3.5 mm: circular 16 in / 40 cm

GAUGE
24 sts = 4 in / 10 cm.
Adjust needle size to obtain correct gauge if necessary.

TECHNIQUE
This double-layered scarf is knitted in
the round following the chart.

Knitting Tips:

For a more even pattern when knitting with two strands
held at the same time over your index finger (continental
method), work as follows: Place the non-dominant
color of the repeat nearest you on your index finger. For
example, first repeat: place the Burnt Orange lower down
on your finger, with Putty on top, near the fingernail.
Work with yarns held in that sequence for 5 rounds. For
the next 6 rounds, hold Putty lower down your index
finger and Burnt Orange near your nail. Change back
to the original order for the last 5 rounds of pattern.

SCARF
With Color 4, CO 149 sts. Join, being careful not to
twist cast-on sts; pm for beginning of rnd.
Knit 8 rnds and then change to MC and knit 16 rnds.
Now work in pattern following chart. *Begin with
CC3.
Work one pattern repeat and then knit 16 rnds with
MC.
Work a new pattern repeat with CC1, knit 16 rnds
with MC, pattern repeat with CC2, knit 16 rnds
with MC*.
Rep * to * 4 times or to desired length. End with 8
rnds CC4. Leave sts on needle.

FINISHING
Turn scarf inside out and weave in all ends neatly on
WS.
With WS facing out, seam scarf along cast-on row.
Turn scarf right side out and divide sts onto two
needles with 75 sts on one needle and 74 sts on
other needle.
Join the sets of sts with Kitchener st, cut yarn and
draw through rem st. Weave in end to inside as
invisibly as possible.
Steam press scarf hard: Dampen a kitchen towel well
and lay scarf so that steam iron does not have
direct contact with scarf. Steam evenly on both
sides so that the scarf becomes totally flat and
the side edges are well defined.

Factory founder Johan E. K. Ramm was knowledgeable about colors.

Here is a typical pattern for factory-produced workers' sweaters, with alternating squares and small crosses. This would have been knitted by hand in school as an example of a simple colorwork pattern, and there are several mittens with this pattern in Norwegian museums. One such pair of children's mittens from Hallingdal is shown in the edition of Annichen Sibbern Bøhn's *Norwegian Knitting Designs* published in 1933. This pattern is also featured on several designs from *Husfliden* (The Norwegian Folk Art and Craft Association), based on hand knitting patterns from Viksdalen and Voss in western Norway.[15] At Salhus Tricotagefabrik, it was in production from about 1910 until 1930, and perhaps even earlier, before it became popular again in the 1970s and '80s.

For our version, the pattern is placed on a modern "Icelander" with many smart details, such as patterning on the raglan shaping and elegant color changes along the way, where the pattern color becomes the main color. The model has a modern look but retro color choice, and is easy and fun to knit. With its pop of yellow, it was named after the dye master Johan Ernst Kristian Ramm (1824-1879) who founded Salhus Tricotagefabrik together with Phillip Christian Clausen.

Knitted samples from around 1920.

This pattern was knitted up in a number of colors around 1920 and made a comeback in the 1970s.

DESIGN
Birger Berge

SKILL LEVEL
Experienced

SIZES
S (M, L, XL, XXL)

FINISHED MEASUREMENTS
Chest: 35½ (39½, 43¼, 47¼, 51¼) in /
90 (100, 110, 120, 130) cm
Total Length: approx. 32¼ (33, 34, 34¾, 35½) in /
82 (84, 86, 88, 90) cm
Sleeve Length: 22½ (23¼, 23¼, 23¾, 23¾) in /
57 (59, 59, 60, 60) cm

MATERIALS
Yarn:
CYCA #2 (sport, baby), Rauma Finull PT2 (100%
Norwegian wool, 191 yd/175 m / 50 g)

Yarn Colors and Amounts:
Color 1: Natural White 401: 150 (200, 200, 250, 250) g
Color 2: Charcoal Gray 414: 150 (150, 200, 200, 250) g
Color 3: Yellow 450: 100 (100, 100, 150, 150) g

Needles:
U. S. sizes 1.5 and 4 / 2.5 and 3.5 mm: circulars
32 or 40 in / 80 or 100 cm; sets of 5 dpn

GAUGE
26 sts on larger needles = 4 in / 10 cm.
Adjust needle size to obtain correct gauge if necessary.

BODY

With Color 3 and smaller circular, CO 214 (242, 266, 290, 318) sts. Join, being careful not to twist cast-on row; pm for beginning of rnd. Work around in k1, p1 ribbing for 20 rnds.

Change to larger circular and knit 1 rnd.

On the next rnd, increase 22 sts evenly spaced around = 236 (264, 288, 312, 340) sts.

K117 (131, 143, 155, 169) for front, p1, k117 (131, 143, 155, 169) for back, p1. **Note:** The pattern will not end up divided evenly by the purl st at the side.

Count out from the X on Chart 1 to determine the center of the front and back. Make sure pattern is centered on each section. Continue purl st up each side as est. Work following Chart 1 until body measures 16½ (17, 17¼, 18¼ 18½) in / 42 (43, 44, 46, 47) cm, ending at A on the chart.

Shape underarms: BO 6 sts on each side of each purl st and also BO the purl st.

SLEEVES

With Color 3 and smaller dpn, CO 42 (44, 44, 46, 48) sts. Divide sts onto dpn and join. Work around in k1, p1 ribbing for 20 rnds.

Change to larger dpn (or needles to obtain gauge). With Color 1, knit 1 rnd. Always purl last st for center of underarm. Knit 1 more rnd, increasing 12 sts evenly spaced around = 54 (56, 56, 58, 60) sts.

Place charted pattern so that the st marked with X is at center sleeve.

On every 5th rnd, increase 1 st on each side of centered purl st on underarm until st count is 108 (100, 114, 118, 122) and sleeve measures 22½ (23¼, 23¼, 23¾, 23¾) in / 57 (59, 59, 60, 60) cm above cast-on row.

End at A on the chart.

Shape underarm as on body (= BO center 13 sts of underarm).

Set sleeve aside while you knit the second sleeve the same way.

RAGLAN SHAPING

Knit around on body to nearest armhole and then knit one sleeve onto same needle. Knit back and then second sleeve = 382 (414, 446, 478, 514) sts.

Pm at each intersection of body and sleeve with 3 sts between markers at each intersection.

Work 1 pattern rep without decreasing. Next, switch colors so Color 2 is now the MC and Color 3 is the CC. The 3 sts between raglan markers are now worked following Chart 2.

Raglan Shaping:

Decrease for raglan on each side of markers at joins, placing the decreases where indicated on Chart 2, always using MC for decreases.

At each intersection: Knit until 2 sts before first marker, k2tog. Follow Chart 2 for sts between decreases. Ssk (or sl 1, k1 psso) = 8 sts decreased per rnd.

Decrease the same way on every other rnd until piece measures 22½ (23¼, 24, 24¾, 25½) in / 57 (59, 61, 63, 65) cm.

NECKBAND

Place 26 sts at center front on a holder.

Now raise back neck as you continue in pattern and work back and forth with raglan shaping.

Round the neckline at center front by placing 8, 6, 4, 2, 2 sts at each side of the 26 front neck sts on a holder. Continue in pattern until piece measures 24½ (24½, 26, 26¾, 27½) in / 62 (62, 66, 68, 70) cm.

Knit 1 rnd over all the sts around front and back neck, *at the same time* decreasing evenly spaced around to 94 (104, 1114, 124, 134) sts.

Change to Color 3 and smaller circular and work around in k1, p1 ribbing for 10 rnds. BO in ribbing.

FINISHING

Fold neckband in half and sew down smoothly on WS.

Seam underarms. Weave in all ends neatly on WS.

Gently steam press sweater under damp pressing cloth or pat out sweater to finished measurements on a damp towel. Cover with another damp towel and leave until completely dry.

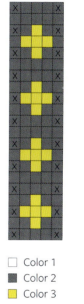

Chart 1 **Chart 2**

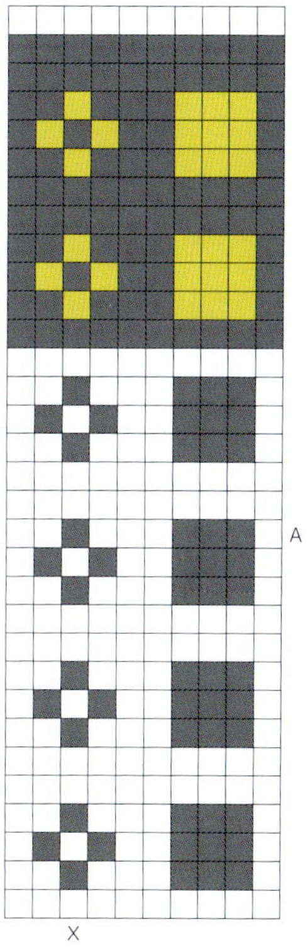

☐ Color 1
■ Color 2
▨ Color 3
⊠ Raglan decrease

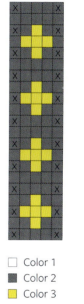

Master Carder

UNISEX PULLOVER

This is perhaps what an "Icelander" produced at Salhus in 1962 might have looked like. The motif is similar to *sjóormurin* ("the sea serpent"), from Hans M. Debes' collection of Faroese knitting patterns. However, in this case the blocks and stripes are multiples of three rather than two as in the original Salhus Tricotagefabrik samples. The inspiration from Faroese fishermen's sweaters is nevertheless unmistakable. Here you can see an attractive pullover inspired by the old workers' sweaters, which were also worn by those working in forestry and at sea. It's knitted on large needles in Fritidsgarn from Sandnes Garn, and is a lovely warm pullover for both women and men. We named it for the carding master at the factory—a man we believe would have had good use for such a solid wool sweater.

Knitted samples from 1962.

SKILL LEVEL
Experienced

SIZES
S (M, L, XL, XXL)

FINISHED MEASUREMENTS
Chest: 37½ (41¼, 45¼, 49¼, 53¼) in /
95 (105, 115, 125, 135) cm
Total Length: 24½ (26½, 28¾, 30, 31) in /
62 (67, 73, 76, 79) cm
Sleeve Length: 18½ (19¼, 20, 20, 21) in /
47 (49, 51, 51, 53) cm

MATERIALS
Yarn:
CYCA #5 (bulky), Sandnes Garn Fritidsgarn
(100% wool, 77 yd/70 m / 50 g)

Yarn Colors and Amounts:
MC: Light Natural White Heather 2641:
350 (400, 450, 500, 550) g
CC1: Olive Green 9336: 50 (50, 50, 50, 50) g
CC2: Beige Heather 2650: 50 (50, 50, 50, 50) g
CC3: Brown Heather 4071: 250 (300, 350, 400, 450) g

Needles:
U. S. size 10 / 6 mm: circulars 16, 24, and 32
in / 40, 60, and 80 cm; set of 5 dpn
U. S. size 8 / 5 mm: circulars 16 and 32 in / 40
and 80 mm; set of 5 dpn (for ribbing)

GAUGE
16 sts x 17 rnds in pattern on larger
needles = 4 x 4 in / 10 x 10 cm.
Adjust needle size to obtain correct gauge if necessary.

BODY

With CC1 and smaller circular, CO 152 (168, 184, 200, 216) sts. Join, being careful not to twist cast-on row; pm for beginning of rnd. Cut CC1 and join MC. Work around in k1, p1 ribbing for 2½ in / 6 cm.

Change to larger circular and work in pattern following Chart 1 until body measures approx. 15¾ (16¼, 17, 17¾, 18½) in / 40 (41, 43, 45, 47) cm.

Continue to chart row marked "BO for underarm on this row."

Pm on 1st and 77th (85th, 93rd, 101st, 109th) st to mark center st of each underarm.

BO 7 sts on each side of each marker (on row indicated on chart).

Set body aside while you knit sleeves.

SLEEVES

With CC1 and smaller dpn, CO 32 (34, 36, 38, 40) sts. Divide sts onto dpn and join. Cut CC1 and join MC. Work around in k1, p1 ribbing for 2½ in / 6 cm.

Change to larger dpn and work in pattern following Chart 1. Count out from arrow for center of sleeve to determine beginning st for your size. Make sure pattern is centered on sleeve. **Note:** Always purl the last st of rnd = center of underarm.

Every ¾ (¾, ¾, ⅝, ⅝) in / 2 (2, 2, 1.5, 1.5) cm, increase 1 st on each side of center purl st until there are 64 (72, 72, 80, 80) sts. Work new sts into pattern. Change to short circular when sts will fit around.

When sleeve measures approx. 18½ (19¼, 20, 20, 21) in / 47 (49, 51, 51, 53) cm, continue to chart row marked "BO for underarm on this row."

BO 7 sts centered on underarm.

Set sleeve aside while you knit second sleeve the same way.

YOKE with RAGLAN SHAPING

Arrange all the pieces on larger circular = 252 (284, 300, 332, 348) sts total.

Knit Row 1 of Chart 2 for yoke. On next rnd, increase with M1 and pm at each intersection of body and sleeve. The new sts (raglan line sts) divide the sleeves and body and *should always be worked with MC.*

The stitch count is now 256 (288, 304, 336, 352). Begin rnd at the first raglan line and follow the instructions for your size below for raglan shaping.

After completing all raglan decreases 80 (80, 80, 88, 88) sts rem. End on pattern row indicated on chart.

Knit 1 rnd with MC and, *at the same time,* decrease 12 (8, 4, 10, 10) sts evenly spaced around = 68 (72, 76, 78, 78) sts rem.

RAGLAN SHAPING

Note: Raglan line sts are always worked in MC. The patterning on each side of a line st is always mirror-image.

Raglan line sts: k2tog, *knit until 2 sts before next raglan line, ssk (or sl 1, k1 in pattern, psso), raglan line st, k2tog*.

Rep * to * at each raglan line.

Decrease for raglan shaping on *every* rnd 5 (7, 9, 9, 11) times. Now decrease on *every other* rnd 17 (19, 19, 22, 22) times.

NECKBAND

Change to smaller short circular and work 3 rnds in k1, p1 ribbing. Change to CC1 and work 6 rnds k1, p1 ribbing. BO knitwise.

FINISHING

Seam underarms.

Fold neckband in half and sew down edge loosely on WS with overhand sts.

Weave in all ends neatly on WS.

Lay sweater, patted out to finished measurements, between two damp towels and leave flat until completely dry.

Chart 1—Body and Sleeves

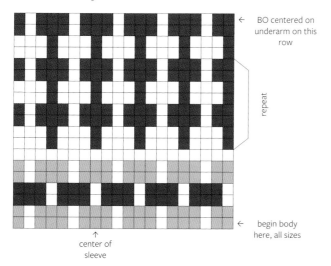

← BO centered on underarm on this row

repeat

← begin body here, all sizes

↑ center of sleeve

Chart 2—Yoke

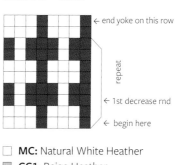

← end yoke on this row

repeat

← 1st decrease rnd

← begin here

☐ **MC:** Natural White Heather
▨ **CC1:** Beige Heather
■ **CC2:** Brown Heather

Some Hillesvåg yarns may be purchased (with international shipping charges) from:

Ysolda

ysolda.com

Rauma yarns are available from:

The Yarn Guys

theyarnguys.com

Some Sandnes yarns may be purchased (with international shipping charges) from:

Scandinavian Knitting Design

scandinavianknittingdesign.com

Additional Sandnes yarns are also available from:

The Loopy Ewe

theloopyewe.com

Some yarns may be difficult to find. A variety of additional and substitute yarns are available from:

Webs – America's Yarn Store

75 Service Center Road
Northampton, MA 01060
800-367-9327
yarn.com

LoveKnitting.com

loveknitting.com/us

If you are unable to obtain any of the yarn used in this book, it can be replaced with a yarn of a similar weight and composition. Please note, however, the finished projects may vary slightly from those shown, depending on the yarn used. Try www.yarnsub.com for suggestions.

For more information on selecting or substituting yarn, contact your local yarn shop or an online store; they are familiar with all types of yarns and would be happy to help you. Additionally, the online knitting community at Ravelry.com has forums where you can post questions about specific yarns. Yarns come and go so quickly these days and there are so many beautiful yarns available.

Acknowledgments

Test Knitters

Janett Vatle Berentzen, Anne Bjørke, Aud Breivik, Tone Brekke, Elisabeth Garmann, Torgun Gjefsen, Renata Gulljord, Margunn Heggernes, Christel Krossøy, Kate Larsen, Gunn Sissel Leithaug, Mona Nilsen, Møyfrid Olsen, Kristine Løken Rognerud, Asbjørg Røneid-Hansen and Inger Marie Aalstad.

Models

Liesa Berens, Imre Kristian and Timea Kristine Ramstrøm Forrás, Ida Areklett Garmann, Harald Gunnarsen, Ingeborg Usin Haugrønning, Eirin Hillestad, Knut Lervåg, Laura Moberg, Marte Maardalen, Ingvil Myklebust Skofteland and Anne-Grethe Bræin Sørensen.

Sponsors

Many thanks to our sponsors: Hillesvåg Ullvarefabrikk, Rauma Garn and Sandnes Garn, for all the beautiful yarn they contributed for us to use in the patterns in this book:

Gry Geelmuyden and Gunn Elin Myhre at Sandnes Garn; Berit Løkken at Hillesvåg Ullvarefabrikk and Hildegard Halse Digneres Rauma Ullvarefabrikk.

Literature

Djuve, Pål H. «Dra te Salhus» – en etnologisk undersøkelse av forenings- og organisasjonsliv med
eksempler og empiri frå Salhus og Mjølkeråen [Go to Salhus! An Ethnological Survey of Associations and Organizations with Examples and Empirical Evidence from Salhus and Mjølkeråen]. Unpublished PhD thesis. University of Bergen. 1982.

Kjellberg, Anne, Ingebjørg Gravjord et. al. Strikking i Norge [Knitting in Norway]. Oslo: The Norwegian Folk Art and Craft Association, Landbruksforlaget. 1987.

Hasle, Kari Aslaug. Frå tale til tekst – om kjønn i arbeid og familie [From Speech to Text – On Gender at Work and in the Family]. Unpublished thesis at a second-degree level. University of Bergen. 1998.

Ramstrøm, Ann Kristin. «Mellom synåla og akkorden – dei fleksible sydamene på Salhus Tricotagefabrik» [«Between the Needle and the Piece Rate – The Flexible Seamstresses at Salhus Tricotagefabrik»],
in Arbeiderhistorie 2015, p. 158–177. Oslo: The Norwegian Labour Movement Archives and Library, 2015. http://www.arbark.no/Arbeiderhistorie/Arbeiderhistorie_2015.htm

Knutsen, Jostein. Nedbygging og nedlegging i tekstilindustrien på Vestlandet – Arne fabrikker og Salhus
Tricotagefabrik. [«Decline and Closures in the Textile Industry in Western Norway – Arne Fabrikker and Salhus Tricotagefabrik»] Unpublished master's thesis. University of Bergen. 2009. http://hdl.handle.net/1956/4730

Sources

Primary Sources

Norsk Folkemuseum, Oslo. Knitted garments from the museum collection.

The Norwegian Knitting Industry Museum, The Museum Centre in Hordaland. Archive materials. BBA/A-1619 Salhus Tricotagefabrik. 1859–1989.

The Norwegian Knitting Industry Museum, The Museum Centre in Hordaland. Knitted samples and objects from Salhus Tricotagefabrik, 1859 – 1989. Interview with workers at Salhus Tricotagefabrik. 1991, 1996, 2009.

The Norwegian Industrial Property Office's database. 24.04.2018. www.patentstyret.no

The National Archives of Norway, Production and industrial statistics, Salhus

Tricotagefabrik. RAA/S-2235, the archives of Statistics Norway.

The Regional State Archives of Bergen, A-32601 Hamre police dept., 12.1 Protocol of assessments of fire insurance, 1854–1872.

Printed Sources

Bratland, Kenneth. Åsane – i fortid og nåtid, book IV [Åsane – In Past and Present Times]. Bergen: Bodoni forlag, 2010.

Bøhn, Annichen Sibbern. Norske strikkemønstre [Norwegian Knitting Patterns]. Oslo: Grøndahl, 1933.

Debes, Hans M. Føroysk bindingamynstur [Faroese Knitting Patterns]. Tórshavn: Føroyskt heimavirki, (1932), 1969 (3rd ed.)

Fasting, Kåre. «Salhus blir industristed» [Salhus Becomes an Industrial Town], in Salhus i gamal
og ny tid [Salhus in Old and New Times], ed. Nils Fotland. p. 133–134. Bergen: Grieg, 1945.

Forrás, Peter. «Vi behøver ikke passe paa arbeideren, vi passer kun paa arbeidet». Arbeid og rasjonalisering
i Salhus Tricotagefabrik 1920–1967 [«We don't have to look after the worker, we only look after the work.» Work and rationalization at Salhus Tricotagefabrik 1920–1967]. Salhus: The Norwegian Knitting Industry Museum, The Museum Centre in Hordaland, 2009.

Grieg, Sigurd. Norsk Tekstil [Norwegian Textiles], book I and II. Oslo: Johan Grundt Tanum, 1948.

Gursli-Berg, Gunhild og Edvard Thorup (eds). Industrispor – frå Melbu til Lindesnes [«Industrial Remains – from Melbu to Lindesnes»]. Oslo: Aschehoug, 2008.

Leicester City Museums Service et al. Knitting Together – The Heritage of the East Midlands Knitting Industry. www.knittingtogether.org.uk

Låstad, Einar. Historik over A/S Salhus Tricotagefabriks virksomhet 1859–1984 [«History of A/S Salhus Tricotagefabrik's Operations 1859–1984»], Åsane: Åsane Trykkeri, 1984.

Pasanen, Merri. Med en nål – bli kjent med nålebinding [«With One Needle – Get Acquainted with Needle Binding»]. Kristiansand: Vest-Agder-museet, 2017.

Småland, Erik. «Salhus – fabrikkstaden ved fjorden» [«Salhus – The Factory Town by the Fjord»] Unpublished article. www.muho.no/wp-content/uploads/2010/09/salhus_fabrikkstaden.pdf

– «Salhus ferjekai» [«Salhus Ferry Quay»]. Unpublished article. 2000. /www.muho.no/wp-content/uploads/2010/09/salhus_ferjekai.pdf

Sundbø, Annemor. *Everyday Knitting – Treasures from a Rag Pile*. Oslo: Samlaget, 1994

– *Strikking i billedkunsten – Knitting in Art*. Kristiansand: Torridal Tweed, 2010.

Teigland, Svein Helge. *Teknologi, ressurser og arbeidere i norsk trikotasjeindustri – «Firma J. Ramm & Clausen» og «Salhus Tricotagefabrik AS» 1859–1900* [*Technology, Resources and Workers in the Norwegian Knitwear Industry – "Firma J. Ramm & Clausen" and "Salhus Tricotagefabrik AS" 1859–1900*]. Unpublished thesis at a second-degree level, University of Bergen. 1994.

Tjersland, Anne Cecilie. «Spøtakoner og strikkemaskiner – en strikketradisjon på Jæren» [«*Knitting Women and their Knitting Machines – A Tradition at Jæren*»], in *Sjå Jæren – årbok for Jærmuseet 2016* [See Jæren – Yearbook for Jærmuseet 2016]. Stavanger: Gunnarshaug Trykkeri, 2016.

Vestlandske Husflidslag (The Western Norwegian Folk Art and Craft Association) *Vestlandsk husflid gjennom 100 år: 1895–1945* [*Western Norwegian Crafts Through 100 years: 1895–1945*]. Bergen: Vestlandske Husflidslag, 1948.

Photos and Illustrations

Tove Lise Mossestad Photography of newly-knitted garments on models and illustration photos pages 8, 28, 29, 31, 34, 36-37, 40, 42, 46, 48, 52-3, 56, 58-9, 62, 64, 66, 70, 72, 74, 76, 79, 86, 88-9, 92, 94, 96, 98, 102, 104-5, 108, 110, 112, 118, 120, 122, 124, 127, 130, 134, 136, 138-9, 142, 144-5, 148, 150, 156, 158 (at left), 162, 164-5, 167, 168, 170, 173, 175-6, 179, 182, 184-5, 190.

Bevaringstenestene (MuHo) Photos of items and some of the knitted samples on pages 15, 26, 28, 39, 45, 61, 85, 97, 101, 113, 123, and 187.

Hanne Dale, Norwegian Knitting Industry Museum (MuHo) Photos of knitted samples, machines, and single garments on pages 6, 12, 13, 16, 23 (lower), 35, 41, 44, 47, 53, 57, 61, 63, 75, 80-82, 87, 97, 103, 109, 114-16, 119, 126, 131, 132, 137, 143, 149, 157, 158 (at right), 160, 177-8, 183, 188.

Helge Sunde Photos of seamstresses in the factory at top of page 16 and Salhus with the Norwegian Knitting Industry Museum, page 17.

Dianna Walla Knitted sample page 150.

Historic Photos

pages 10, 14, 16, 24, 75, 119, 149, and 177: photos from the archives at Salhus Tricotagefabrik, unknown photographer.

page 18: advertisement posters and signs from the archive at Salhus Tricotagefabrik, unknown artist.

page 20: advertisement poster for Salhus Tricotagefabrik, produced by Høydahl Ohme advertising firm, Oslo, Norway.

pages 21-23: advertisement posters and signs from the archive at Salhus Tricotagefabrik, unknown photographer/artist.

page 25; Advertisement booklet for "Bi" knitting machine, Hjemmeindustri AS, unknown artist.

Notes

1   Fasting, Kåre. «Salhus blir industristed», p. 133–134.
2   The Regional State Archives of Bergen, Hamre police dept., 12.1 Protocol of assessments of fire insurance
3   Teigland, Teknologi, ressurser og arbeidere [...], p. 22.
4   Fasting, Kåre, «A/S Salhus Tricotagefabrik 1859–1944» in Historik over Salhus Tricotagefabriks 125 års virksomhet. p. 22–27.
5   The National Archives of Norway, Production and industrial statistics, SalhusTricotagefabrik.
6   From the English word shoddy, materials for spinning made of reclaimed wool.
7   Forrás, Peter, «Vi behøver ikke passe paa arbeideren (...)», p. 20. The National Archives of Norway, Production and industrial statistics, Salhus Tricotagefabrik, RAA/S-2235.
8   So-called "Icelander" sweaters (Islender in Norwegian) may actually have originated in the Faroe Islands, where sweaters with similar small, two-color motifs were common. It's possible that importation of Faroese sweaters made in Icelandic wool created the Norwegian association between these sweaters and Iceland.
9   The Norwegian Industrial Property Office's database, 02.01.2018.
10   Bergen City Archives, A-1619 Salhus Tricotagefabrik, Hi Sales and production.
11   Archive materials from Dovre at The Norwegian Museum of Science and Technology, Oslo.
12   See for instance Tjersland's article «Spøtakoner og strikkemaskiner – en strikketradisjon på Jæren» [«Knitting Women and their Knitting Machines – A Tradition at Jæren»].
13   Bratland, Kenneth. Åsane – i fortid og nåtid IV [«Åsane – In Past and Present Times»], p. 118.
14   Bratland, Kenneth. Åsane – i fortid og nåtid IV, p. 203.
15   Bratland, Kenneth. Åsane – i fortid og nåtid IV, p. 69.
16   See e.g. Sundbø, Annemor 1994, p. 64, Annichen Sibbern Bøhn 1933, p. 20–21 and Vestlandske Husflidslag (The Western Norwegian Folk Art and Craft Association) 1948, p. 100. The knitted jackets referred to are models no. 3 and 82.